Explore THE UNITED STATES

History

History is the story of people and places from the past.

Welcome to the
Gila Cliff Dwellings
in New Mexico

Mogollon (muh-gee-YOHN) people built the cliff dwellings more than 700 years ago. These homes show what life was like in ancient times. **Ancient** means from a very long time ago.

Gila Cliff
Dwellings
■ National
Monument

Fast Fact:

The Mogollon did not live in the dwellings very long. Nobody knows why they left their homes.

The dwellings became a national monument in 1907. They are preserved so we can learn how people lived in the past. **Preserve** is to keep something from being harmed or changed.

The Mogollons made clay pots and tools.

Link to You

Describe something you have seen or learned about that is ancient.

Economics

Economics is the study of money, goods, and services.

Welcome to the Crayon Factory

in Easton, Pennsylvania

Crayons are goods. **Goods** are things people make or grow. Visitors to the factory learn how crayons are made.

First, wax and color are heated together. The wax and color are put into a mold.

After the crayon cools, it gets a label.

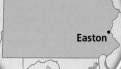

Easton

Next, the crayons are put in a box. The boxes are then shipped to stores.

People buy the crayons. **Buy** means to use money to get something.

Fast Fact:

The first crayons to be used by school children were made in 1903.

Link to You

Where would you go to buy crayons? What other goods could you buy there?

Science and Technology

Science and Technology can change the way we live.

Welcome to O'Hare International Airport in Chicago

Air-traffic controllers watch planes from the control tower. Special equipment lets air-traffic controllers tell pilots when it is safe for planes to take off or to land. Controllers **communicate**, or exchange information, with the plane's pilot by radio.

Chicago

Pilots need to know about the weather. Computers tell the controller what the weather will be for a plane's trip. A **computer** is a machine that can keep and give back information.

Fast Fact:

O'Hare International Airport is one of the world's busiest airports. More than 900,000 planes take off and land at O'Hare each year.

Link to You

How many different uses for a computer can you think of? Describe them.

E7

Geography

Geography is the study of the Earth and how people use it.

Welcome to Louisville, Kentucky

Louisville is a big city in Kentucky. A **city** is a large town with many people. There are tall buildings in the city. People take cars or ride the bus to get from place to place.

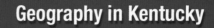

Louisville is in the Bluegrass **region,** or part, of Kentucky. The name comes from the kind of grass that grows there. This region is known for its horse farms. Horse farms are in the country. The **country** is an area with a lot of open land and fewer people.

Fast Fact:

Bluegrass isn't really blue—it's green! In the spring the grass forms small blue flower buds.

Link to You

Think of a city you have visited or read about. How would you describe this city?

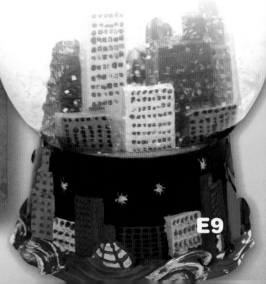

E9

Culture

Culture is made up of the ideas and beliefs of a group of people.

Welcome to New Orleans, Louisiana

Jazz music is a tradition in New Orleans, Louisiana. **Tradition** is the way something has been done for a long time.

Folk art shows the culture and traditions of the people who live in a certain place.

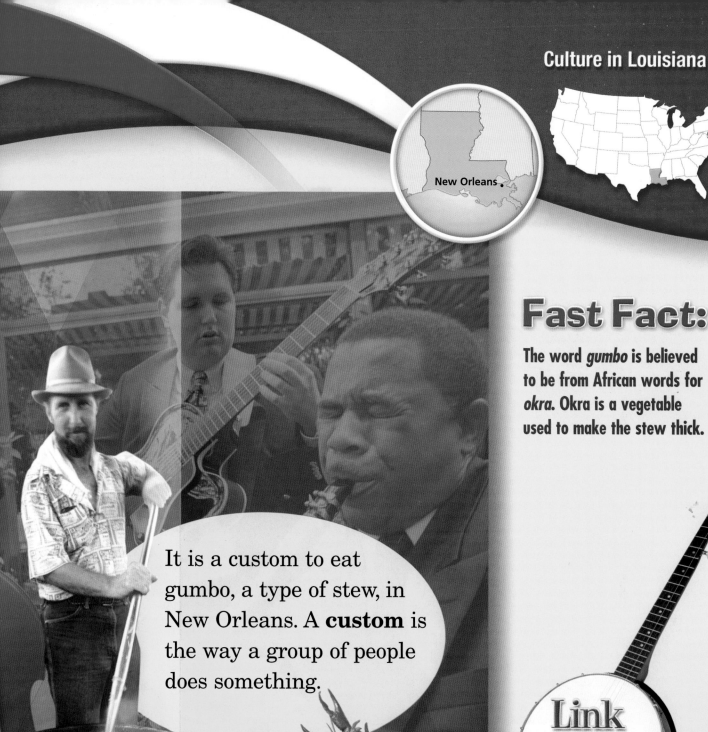

New Orleans

The word *gumbo* is believed to be from African words for *okra*. Okra is a vegetable used to make the stew thick.

It is a custom to eat gumbo, a type of stew, in New Orleans. A **custom** is the way a group of people does something.

Link to You

What are some customs in your community?

Citizenship

Citizenship is the rights and responsibilities of belonging to a nation or community.

Welcome to Anchorage, Alaska

Volunteers help with recycling in Anchorage. A **volunteer** is someone who does something without receiving pay.

Anchorage

People in Anchorage show responsibility by recycling. **Responsibility** is a duty to take care of something.

People work together to sort cans, glass, and plastic.

Recycling Team

Fast Fact:

Alaska has a Flying Cans program. Small communities collect cans that are flown for free to Anchorage for recycling.

Link to You

What responsibilities do you have at home? At school?

E13

Government

Government is a group of people who make laws for our country or state.

The Milwaukee County Courthouse was built in 1929. It is a national landmark.

Milwaukee

A courthouse is a government building. Judges work at courthouses. A judge decides whether people are guilty of breaking laws. **Laws** are rules that everyone must obey.

A jury might also decide whether someone has broken the law. A **jury** is a group of people who decide whether someone is guilty or not guilty.

Fast Fact:

Each year on May 1, people in the United States celebrate Law Day.

Link to You

What is one law in your community? What might happen if someone did not obey this law?

E15

National Symbols

The Liberty Bell
Philadelphia

◄ The Liberty Bell was rung when the United States first became a nation. It is a symbol of freedom.

U.S. Currency

▲

The one-dollar bill is United States currency, or money. On the front of the bill is a picture of George Washington. Two circles on the back of the bill show both sides of the Great Seal of the United States.

Bald Eagle

▲

The bald eagle is a large, strong bird. It is a symbol of strength, courage, and freedom.

SCOTT FORESMAN

SOCIAL STUDIES

PEOPLE AND PLACES

PROGRAM AUTHORS

Dr. Candy Dawson Boyd
Professor, School of Education
Director of Reading Programs
St. Mary's College
Moraga, California

Dr. Geneva Gay
Professor of Education
University of Washington
Seattle, Washington

Rita Geiger
Director of Social Studies and
Foreign Languages
Norman Public Schools
Norman, Oklahoma

Dr. James B. Kracht
Associate Dean for Undergraduate
Programs and Teacher Education
College of Education
Texas A&M University
College Station, Texas

Dr. Valerie Ooka Pang
Professor of Teacher Education
San Diego State University
San Diego, California

Dr. C. Frederick Risinger
Director, Professional Development
and Social Studies Education
Indiana University
Bloomington, Indiana

Sara Miranda Sanchez
Elementary and Early Childhood
Curriculum Coordinator
Albuquerque Public Schools
Albuquerque, New Mexico

CONTRIBUTING AUTHORS

Dr. Carol Berkin
Professor of History
Baruch College and the Graduate Center
The City University of New York
New York, New York

Lee A. Chase
Staff Development Specialist
Chesterfield County Public Schools
Chesterfield County, Virginia

Dr. Jim Cummins
Professor of Curriculum
Ontario Institute for Studies in Education
University of Toronto
Toronto, Canada

Dr. Allen D. Glenn
Professor and Dean Emeritus
Curriculum and Instruction
College of Education
University of Washington
Seattle, Washington

Dr. Carole L. Hahn
Professor, Educational Studies
Emory University
Atlanta, Georgia

Dr. M. Gail Hickey
Professor of Education
Indiana University-Purdue University
Fort Wayne, Indiana

Dr. Bonnie Meszaros
Associate Director
Center for Economic Education and
Entrepreneurship
University of Delaware
Newark, Delaware

CONTENT CONSULTANTS

Catherine Deans-Barrett
World History Specialist
Northbrook, Illinois

Dr. Michael Frassetto
Studies in Religions
Independent Scholar
Chicago, Illinois

Dr. Gerald Greenfield
Hispanic-Latino Studies
History Department
University of Wisconsin, Parkside
Kenosha, Wisconsin

Dr. Frederick Hoxie
Native American Studies
University of Illinois
Champaign, Illinois

Dr. Cheryl Johnson-Odim
Dean of Liberal Arts and Sciences and
Professor of History
African American History Specialist
Columbia College
Chicago, Illinois

Dr. Michael Khodarkovsky
Eastern European Studies
University of Chicago
Chicago, Illinois

Robert Moffet
U.S. History Specialist
Northbrook, Illinois

Dr. Ralph Nichols
East Asian History
University of Chicago
Chicago, Illinois

CLASSROOM REVIEWERS

Diana Vicknair Ard
Woodlake Elementary School
St. Tammany Parish
Mandeville, Louisiana

Sharon Berenson
Freehold Learning Center
Freehold, New Jersey

Betsy Blandford
Pocahontas Elementary School
Powhatan, Virginia

Nancy Neff Burgess
Upshur County Schools
Buckhannon-Upshur Middle School
Upshur County, West Virginia

Gloria Cantatore
Public School #5
West New York, New Jersey

Stephen Corsini
Content Specialist in Elementary Social Studies
School District 5 of Lexington
and Richland Counties
Ballentine, South Carolina

Deanna Crews
Millbrook Middle School
Elmore County
Millbrook, Alabama

LuAnn Curran
Westgate Elementary School
St. Petersburg, Florida

Kevin L. Curry
Social Studies Curriculum Chair
Hickory Flat Elementary School
Henry County, McDonough, Georgia

Sheila A. Czech
Sky Oaks Elementary School
Burnsville, Minnesota

Louis De Angelo
Office of Catholic Education
Archdiocese of Philadelphia
Philadelphia, Pennsylvania

Dr. Trish Dolasinski
Paradise Valley School District
Arrowhead Elementary School
Glendale, Arizona

Dr. John R. Doyle
Director of Social Studies Curriculum
Miami-Dade County Schools
Miami, Florida

Dr. Roceal Duke
District of Columbia Public Schools
Washington, D.C.

Peggy Flanagan
Roosevelt Elementary School
Community Consolidated School District #64
Park Ridge, Illinois

Mary Flynn
Arrowhead Elementary School
Glendale, Arizona

Sue Gendron
Spring Branch ISD
Houston, Texas

Su Hickenbottom
Totem Falls Elementary School
Snohomish School District
Snohomish, Washington

Chelle Howatt
Ponte Vedra-Palm Valley School
St. Augustine, Florida

Allan Jones
North Branch Public Schools
North Branch, Minnesota

Martha Sutton Maple
Shreve Island School
Shreveport, Louisiana

Lyn Metzger
Carpenter Elementary School
Community Consolidated School District #64
Park Ridge, Illinois

Marsha Munsey
Riverbend Elementary School
West Monroe, Louisiana

Christine Nixon
Warrington Elementary School
Escambia County School District
Pensacola, Florida

Cynthia K. Reneau
Muscogee County School District
Columbus, Georgia

Brandon Dale Rice
Secondary Education Social Science
Mobile County Public School System
Mobile, Alabama

Liz Salinas
Supervisor
Edgewood ISD
San Antonio, Texas

Beverly Scaling
Desert Hills Elementary
Las Cruces, New Mexico

Madeleine Schmitt
St. Louis Public Schools
St. Louis, Missouri

Barbara Schwartz
Central Square Intermediate School
Central Square, New York

Catherine L. Warren
Carlton Palmore Elementary
Lakeland, Florida

Editorial Offices:
• Glenview, Illinois
• Parsippany, New Jersey
• New York, New York

Sales Offices:
• Parsippany, New Jersey
• Duluth, Georgia
• Glenview, Illinois
• Coppell, Texas
• Ontario, California
• Mesa, Arizona

www.sfsocialstudies.com

ISBN: 0-328-07569-8

2 3 4 5 6 7 8 9 10 V057 13 12 11 10 09 08
07 06 05 04

Contents

Social Studies Handbook

UNIT 1

Where We Live

Our Earth

UNIT 3

Working Together

UNIT 4

Our Country Today

UNIT 5

Our Country Long Ago

UNIT 6

People and Places in History

Reference Guide

Social Studies Handbook

Biographies

Maps

Skills

Citizenship Skills

There are many ways to show good citizenship. In your textbook, you will learn about people who are good citizens in their community, state, and country.

Caring means understanding how someone feels and being thoughtful.

Respect means treating others as you want to be treated.

Responsibility means doing what is expected of you.

Fairness means taking turns and playing by the rules.

Honesty means giving back what isn't yours and telling the truth.

Courage means doing what is right even when it is hard.

★ Citizenship in Action ★

Good citizens learn to solve problems. They make careful decisions. Help these children act like good citizens. Here are the steps they follow.

Problem Solving

It is time to go inside but we cannot find one of the soccer balls. What can we do?

1. Name the problem.
2. Find out more about the problem.
3. List ways to solve the problem.
4. Talk about the best way to solve the problem.
5. Solve the problem.
6. How well is the problem solved?

★ Citizenship in Action ★

Decision Making

We are planning a class party. Which games should we play?

1. Tell what decision you need to make.
2. Gather information.
3. List your choices.
4. Tell what might happen with each choice.
5. Make a decision.

American flag is a symbol of our country. number of stripes on the flag stand for the ber of states there were when the country began. There is one star for each of the tates.

Flag Rules

You should follow these rules when you say the Pledge of Allegiance.

1. First, you should stand.
2. Then, you should face the flag.
3. Next, you should put your right hand over your heart. This shows honor and respect.
4. Last, you should say the Pledge of Allegiance!

The Pledge of Allegiance

I pledge allegiance to the Flag of the United States of America, and to the Republic for which it stands, one Nation under God, indivisible, with liberty and justice for all.

The Star-Spangled Banner

Oh, say! can you see, by the dawn's early light,

What so proudly we hailed at the twilight's
last gleaming?

Whose broad stripes and bright stars, through
the perilous fight,

O'er the ramparts we watched were so
gallantly streaming?

And the rockets' red glare, the bombs
    bursting in air,
Gave proof through the night that our flag
    was still there.
O say, does that Star-Spangled Banner yet wave,
O'er the land of the free and the home of
    the brave?

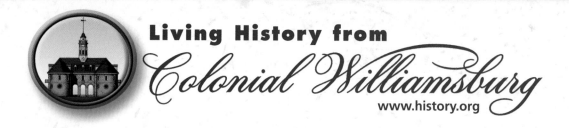

Living History from

Colonial Williamsburg

www.history.org

Think Like a Historian

Historians like to read old letters and papers. They help them learn about life in the past. Do you keep a diary? George Washington did. His diary helps us learn about his life. We can learn what the weather was like at his home in Mount Vernon by looking at his diary.

May 1, 1799
"Morning Cloudy . . ."

May 8, 1799
"Clear, but cool . . ."

May 13, 1799
"Clear & calm all day."

May 31, 1799
". . . rain last night."

We can learn what the weather was like at Mount Vernon by looking at George Washington's diary.

George Washington

You can keep a diary too. Each day write down what the weather is like at your house. Historians might find your diary two hundred years from now. It would help them understand what your life is like.

Keep a Diary

You can keep a diary just like George Washington did. A diary will help you remember your past.

1 Put pages together to make your diary.

2 Next write the month, the day, and the year.

3 Then write down what you would like to remember about the day. You might want to write what is important or special.

August 25, 2003

Today we went to Colonial Williamsburg. It was so much fun! I liked the costumes the people wore.

August 25, 2003

Today we went to Colonial Williamsburg. It was so much fun! I liked the costumes the people wore.

4 You can also include your thoughts or pictures in your diary.

Use Different Resources

There are many different resources you can use to get information. Suppose you want to learn more about the shoes shown on these pages. This type of shoe is called a moccasin.

Encyclopedia

An encyclopedia has information about many topics. The topics are in alphabetical order. You can find out more about moccasins by looking under "M" in the encyclopedia.

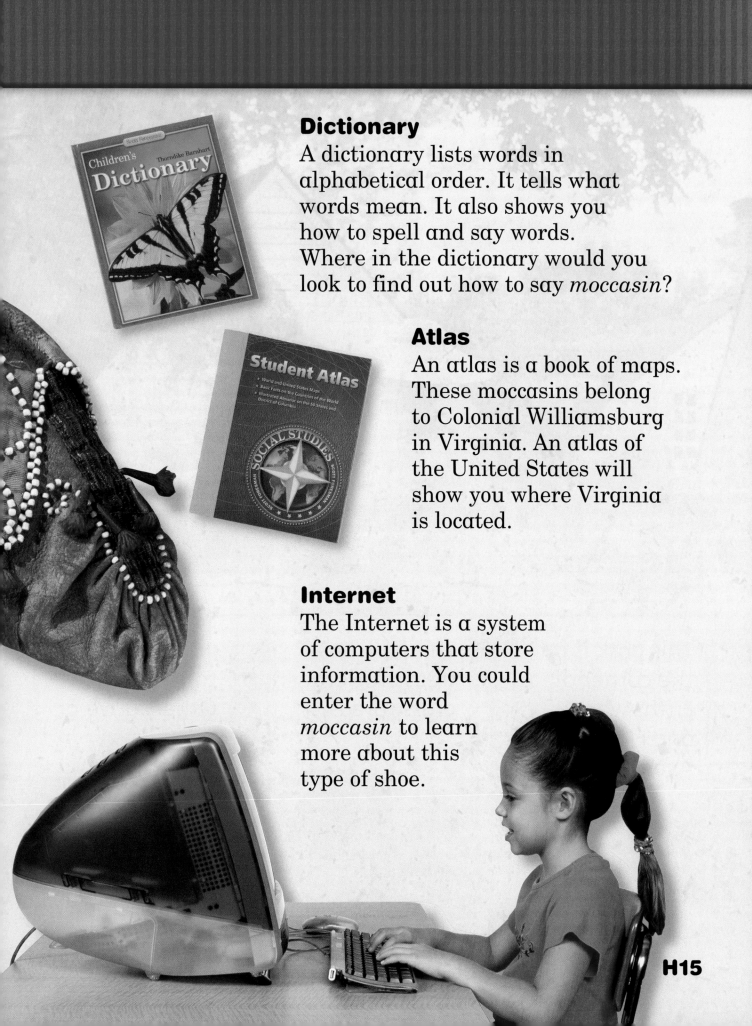

Dictionary

A dictionary lists words in alphabetical order. It tells what words mean. It also shows you how to spell and say words. Where in the dictionary would you look to find out how to say *moccasin*?

Atlas

An atlas is a book of maps. These moccasins belong to Colonial Williamsburg in Virginia. An atlas of the United States will show you where Virginia is located.

Internet

The Internet is a system of computers that store information. You could enter the word *moccasin* to learn more about this type of shoe.

Geography Skills

Five Things to Think About

Geography is the study of Earth. This study sometimes looks at the Earth in five different ways. These ways are called the five themes of geography. Each theme is another way of thinking about an area. Look at the examples of the park below.

Location

Fifth Avenue

Sculpture Park

Flagler Avenue

This park is on the corner of Fifth Avenue and Flagler Avenue.

Place

This park has trees and large grassy areas.

Movement

Some people walk or skate to the park. Others drive or ride bikes.

Places and People Change Each Other

The park has large artwork. Now there are more interesting things to look at than just trees.

Region

This park is in a part of the country that has warm weather for most of the year.

From the Earth to a Globe

Our **Earth** is like a ball floating in space. This picture of Earth was taken from deep space. Earth is made up of land and water.

Vocabulary

Earth
continent
ocean
model
globe

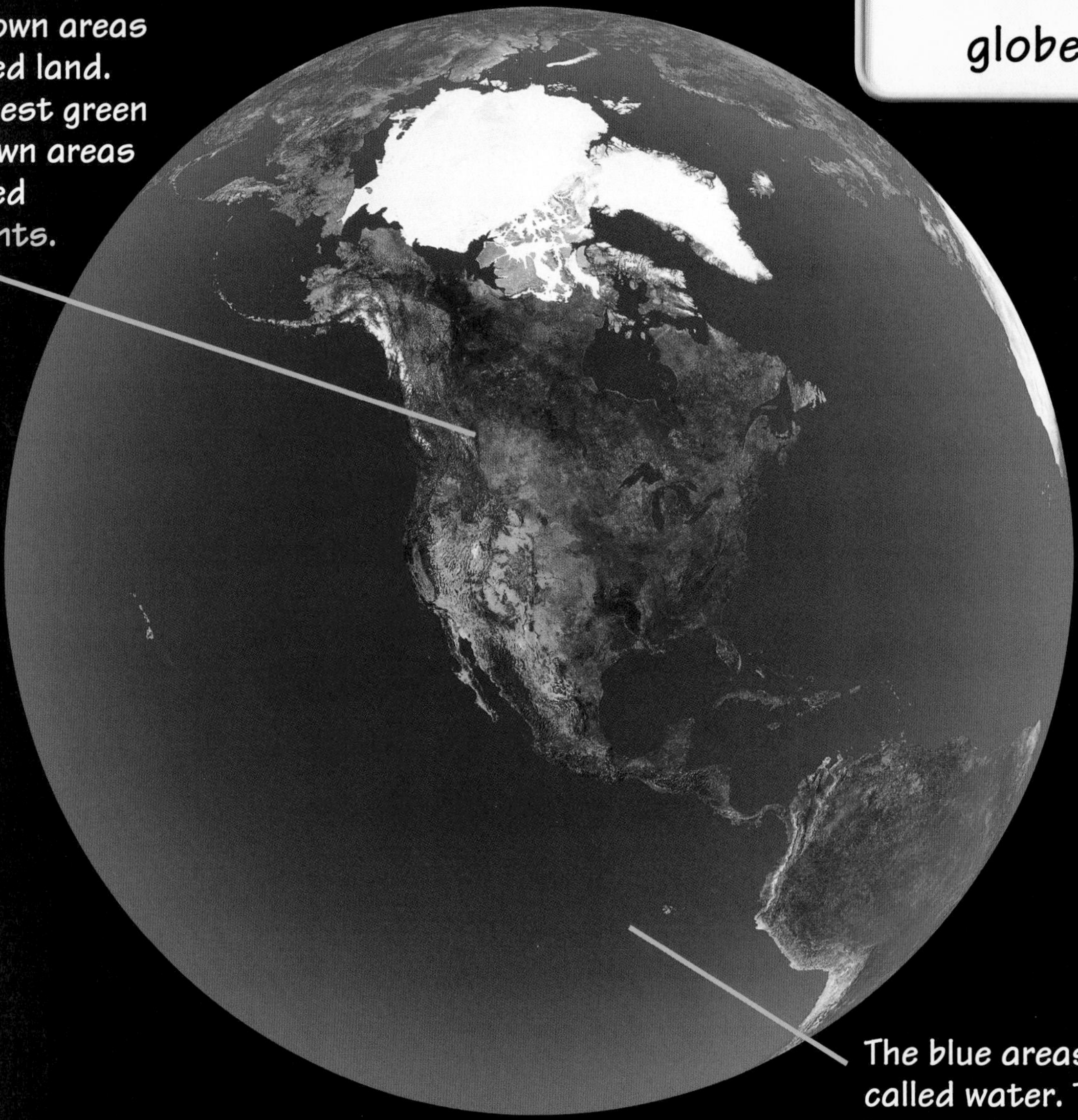

The green and light brown areas are called land. The largest green and brown areas are called continents.

The blue areas are called water. The largest blue areas are called oceans.

You can hold a globe in your hands!

A **model** of Earth is called a **globe.** Globes show the continents and oceans of Earth. You can turn a globe and get an idea of how far away Earth's seven continents are from each other. You can also see how big the oceans are as you turn a globe.

A model is a small copy of something.

How are the picture and map alike? How are they different?

Read a Map

Not all pictures of Earth show the whole planet. The picture above shows only a small part of Earth. This is a farm as seen from above.

It has buildings, fields, and roads. A drawing of this picture is called a map. Look at the map on the next page.

Vocabulary

symbol
map key

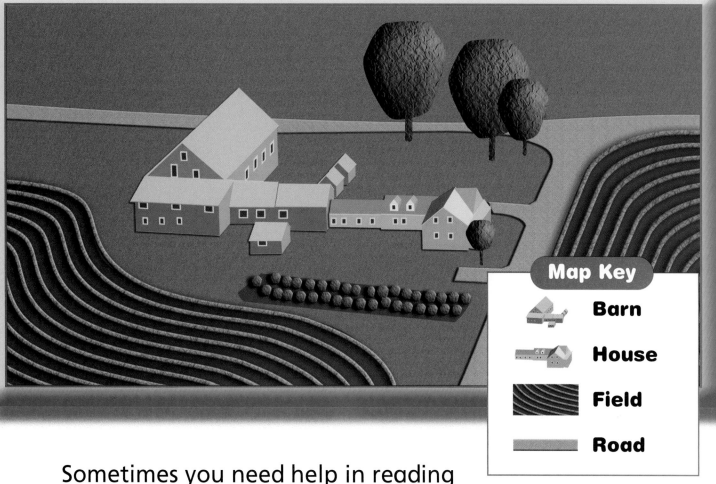

Map Key

Barn

House

Field

Road

What things on the map do the symbols stand for?

Sometimes you need help in reading a map. A **symbol** is a shape, a color, or a line that stands for something. Knowing what the symbols stand for can help you read a map.

A **map key,** or legend, is a box that is part of the map. It is where you will find the symbols. The map key also tells you what the symbols mean, or stand for.

Geography Skills

Read Symbols on Maps

Symbols on maps can show many kinds of things. Here are some examples.

Vocabulary
boundary

Black dots with names are used to show cities. Capital cities are usually shown with a star.

A **boundary,** or border, separates one area or state from another. Boundaries between states or countries are shown with black or gray lines.

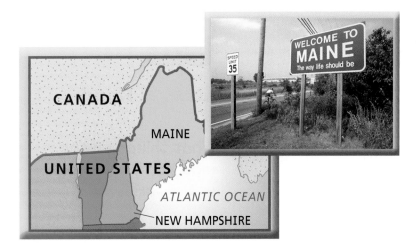

Blue lines with names are sometimes used to show rivers. Sometimes rivers are part of a border.

Maps use lines with names or numbers to show highways.

Here is how maps show railroads.

Look at the map to the right. It shows the five symbols you have just learned.

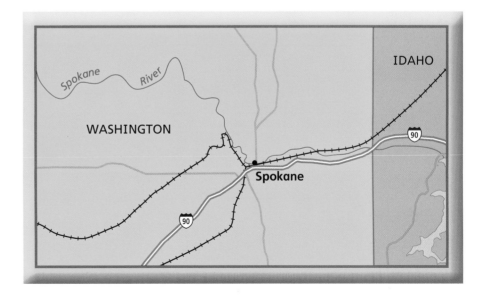

Geography Skills

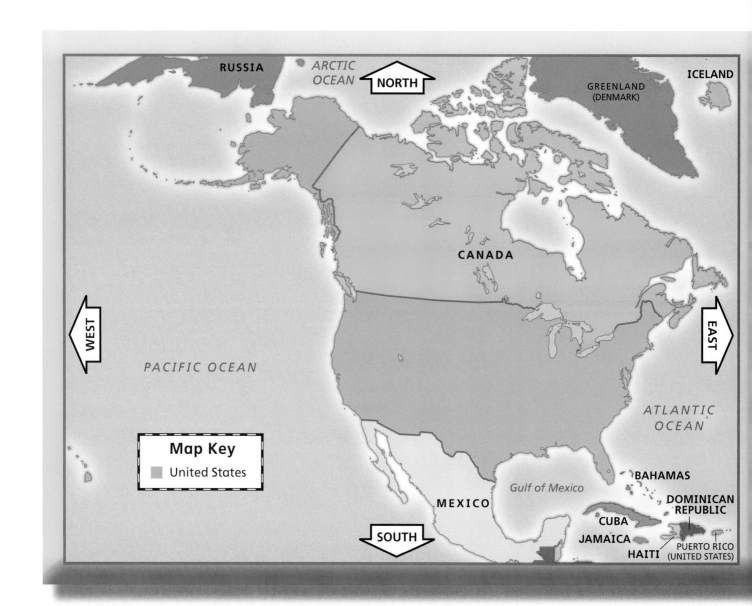

Color on Maps

Remember that color is also a symbol. Color is important for showing things quickly and more clearly. Look at the map above. Color shows you which islands on the map belong to the United States. Does Canada have islands?

Color can make a map brighter and more interesting. Color can also help make it easier to learn from a map. The map of the United States above uses different colors for the states. Which states touch the water of the Gulf of Mexico?

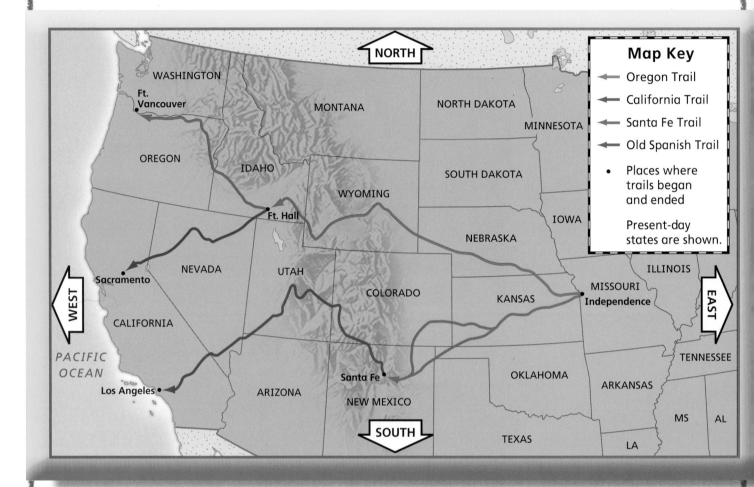

Read a History Map

A history map shows places and events from the past. The map above shows some of the trails people used long ago to move west.

1. What is the longest trail?
2. Which two cities in California were part of a trail?
3. Two trails began in Independence, Missouri. Where did each trail end?

Places Where We Live

by Charlotte Munez

Sung to the tune of
"On Top of Old Smokey"

We live in big cities
And suburbs or towns.
These places are different
In their sights and their sounds.

Big cities and small towns
Are found everywhere.
A road or a highway
Will take you right there!

3

Vocabulary Preview

rural

suburb

urban

Indiana

★ Indianapolis

STOP

law

vote

community

history

What should we do at recess

Play soccer |||
Jump rope |||

Vote Today

urban

suburb

rural

capital

We Belong to Groups

Target skill

Use Context and Picture Clues

Hi! I'm Joanna. I belong to many groups. A **group** is a gathering of people or things. People in a group can do activities together.

If you don't know what a word means, look at the words around it to find some clues. These clues will help you find its meaning.

Mrs. Ward asked the singers to stand together as a group.

6

Pictures can also help you learn the meaning of a word. Look at these pictures. How do they help you learn the meaning of **group?**

Draw a picture of two groups. Tell or write about what people do in each group.

Living in a Neighborhood

My home and school are in my neighborhood. A neighborhood is a place where people live, work, play, and help each other. Look at these pictures of my neighborhood. My neighborhood is a very busy place! What is your neighborhood like?

Our neighborhood has many rules. Rules tell us what to do and what not to do. Rules help keep us safe. What might happen if we did not follow rules?

A rule that everyone must follow is called a **law.** Laws keep our neighborhood safe and clean. What laws do these signs show?

People in our neighborhood help us follow rules and laws. They help keep us safe too.

Every morning, I ride the bus to school. Our bus driver makes sure that we stay in our seats. This is an important rule. What do you think might happen if we did not follow this rule?

We also follow rules in school. Our principal, the leader of our school, makes some of these rules. These rules help us work and play together.

We help our teacher make some of the classroom rules. Today, we voted on a new rule. To **vote** is to make a choice about something. Sometimes, we vote to change a rule to make it better.

What did you learn?

1. Make a list of rules that you follow at home or at school.

2. How do people in your neighborhood follow **laws?** Tell what might happen if people did not follow these laws.

3. **Think and Share** Explain what the word *neighborhood* means. Use words and pictures from the lesson to tell about the meaning of neighborhood.

Kids Care Clubs

The Kids Care Clubs started in New Canaan, Connecticut.

Kids Care Clubs first began when a group of children decided to rake a lawn for a neighbor who was old. Later, these children made lunches to give to a soup kitchen. The children felt good because they were able to help neighbors in need.

Today, more than 25,000 children are part of Kids Care Clubs in the United States and Canada. These children have learned how important it is to help others.

BUILDING CITIZENSHIP
★ Caring
Respect
Responsibility
Fairness
Honesty
Courage

Children in Kids Care Clubs show they care by working on special projects. Some clubs collected food, toys, and blankets for people who lost their homes in an earthquake. One club made bedtime snacks for children in a homeless shelter.

A Kids Care Club at Holmes School in Darien, Connecticut, collected books for other children who needed them. They did this to share their love of reading with others.

★ Caring in Action ★

Think of ways to show that you care about people in your school and neighborhood.

Problem Solving at the Library

Joanna's class read a newspaper story about a problem at their community library. Here are the steps the class took to help solve the problem.

Step 1 Name the problem.

Step 2 Find out more about the problem.

Let's talk to the librarian.

Step 3 List ways to solve the problem.

- **Bring books from home.**
- **Have a bake sale to make money for books.**
- **Collect pennies to buy books.**

Step 4 Is one way more useful than another? Talk about the best way to solve the problem.

Step 5 Solve the problem.

Step 6 How well is the problem solved?

Try it!

1. How did the class show that they cared about their community?

2. List the steps the class took to solve the problem at the library.

3. **On Your Own** Brainstorm ways to help your school or neighborhood. Write your own six-step plan.

A Walk Through a Community

Last summer, my friend, Mike, came to visit my family. We stayed in my own community because there's so much to do!

A **community** is made up of many neighborhoods. I live in New York City, a very large community. We went to Little Italy, Chinatown, and Central Park. Can you find them on my map? Read my journal to find out what we did.

Chinatown

Little Italy

Fifth Avenue

Store

Friday, July 25

I love the food in Little Italy! It was fun listening to people in this neighborhood speak Italian. Mike's family speaks Italian. He said "Ciao" to our server. I said "Hello." We ate a frozen dessert called Italian ice.

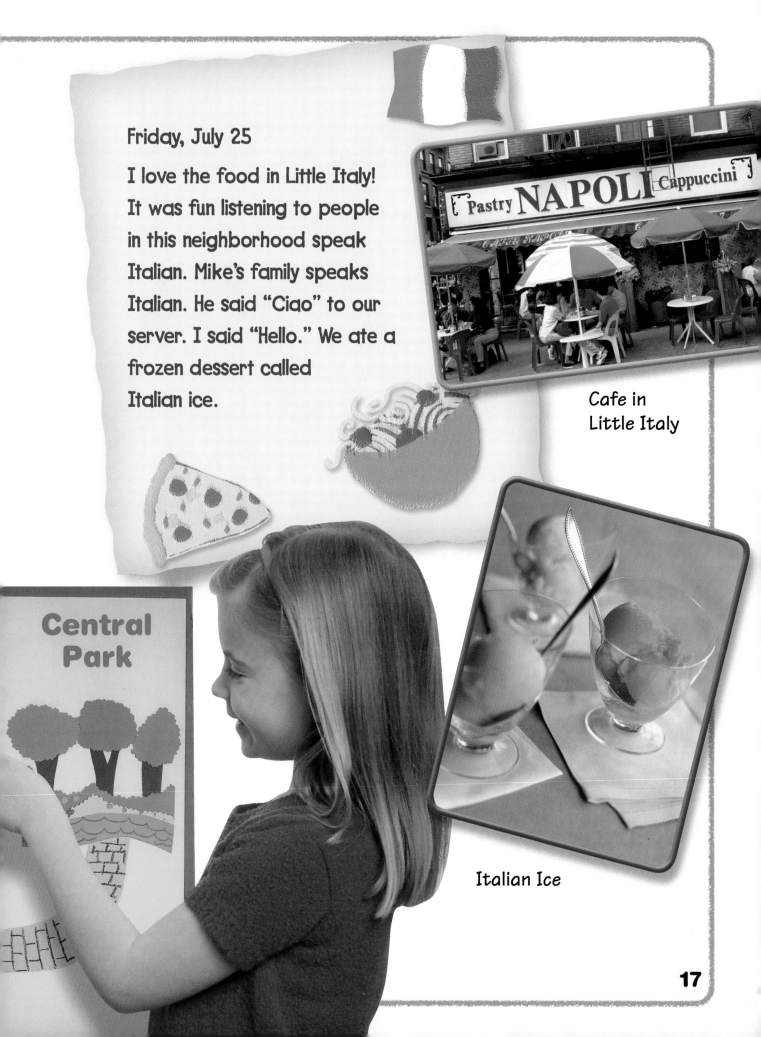

Cafe in Little Italy

Central Park

Italian Ice

Saturday, July 26

Chinatown is a busy neighborhood near Little Italy. My family and I come here often to visit friends, eat, and shop. Mike and I got pretty paper dragons.

We also went to a museum. Here we learned about the culture, or way of life, of Chinese Americans living in New York City and other communities.

Fifth Avenue

Sunday, July 27

Today was busy! First we walked along Fifth Avenue. We saw many tall buildings called skyscrapers.

Next we went to Central Park. We saw people having picnics. While we were at the park, we visited the zoo. Our last stop for the day was the museum.

Central Park

What did you learn?

1. Describe two neighborhoods in Joanna's **community.**

2. Make a list of things you would enjoy doing in New York City.

3. **Think and Share** Draw a picture of Joanna's community. Now draw a picture of your community. How are these two communities alike? How are they different?

Read a City Map

Here is a map and map key of one part of New York City that Joanna and Mike visited. A **map** is a drawing that shows you where places are located. **Symbols** are pictures that stand for things on a map. A **map key** tells what the symbols on a map mean.

North

West

Columbus Avenue

W. 72nd Street

Central Park West

W. 57th Street

E. 79th Stree

Fifth Avenue

E. 72nd Street

Madison Avenue

E. 60th Street

E. 57th Street

South

For more information, go online to the *Atlas* at **www.sfsocialstudies.com.**

Look at the symbols on the map key. Find the symbol for the zoo. Now find the zoo on the map.

Maps have four main directions. Main directions are also called **cardinal directions.** The directions are north, south, east, and west. Find the arrows that show north, south, east, and west on the map.

Map Key

Zoo

Metropolitan Museum of Art

Belvedere Castle

Skyscraper

East

Carnegie Hall

Street/Avenue

Central Park

Path

Lake

Park Ave.

Try it!

1. Tell what a map shows.

2. Is the 🏯 north or south of the 🏢 ?

3. **On Your Own** Draw a map of a park. Include a map key and arrows on the map that show the directions.

How a Community Changes

Look at this picture taken long ago. It shows part of New York's history. **History** tells the story of people, events, and places from the past.

Broadway North from 45th Street, New York City.

22

This is a picture of New York City at the present time. How does this picture look different from the picture taken in the past? How has the city changed?

Hands-on History

Find out what your community was like 100 years ago. What is it like today? How might your community change in the future?

Broadway North from 45th Street, New York City.

23

Lesson 3

Comparing Communities

New York City has become bigger and busier over time. There are more roads and buildings. There are more people too. Urban areas, like New York City, are crowded with people going to work, shopping, and visiting museums or parks. An **urban** area is a city.

In urban communities, many people move around by walking or driving a car. They move around by subway, bus, or taxi too.

24

Many people live in a kind of community called a suburb. A **suburb** is an area located near a city. My friend, Mike, lives in a suburban area. His neighborhood is quieter than mine!

Mike's family moved to a suburb when his mom became the principal of a school there. His dad rides the train to the city to work. Mike's family shops at a shopping mall. Different kinds of stores sell many things they need.

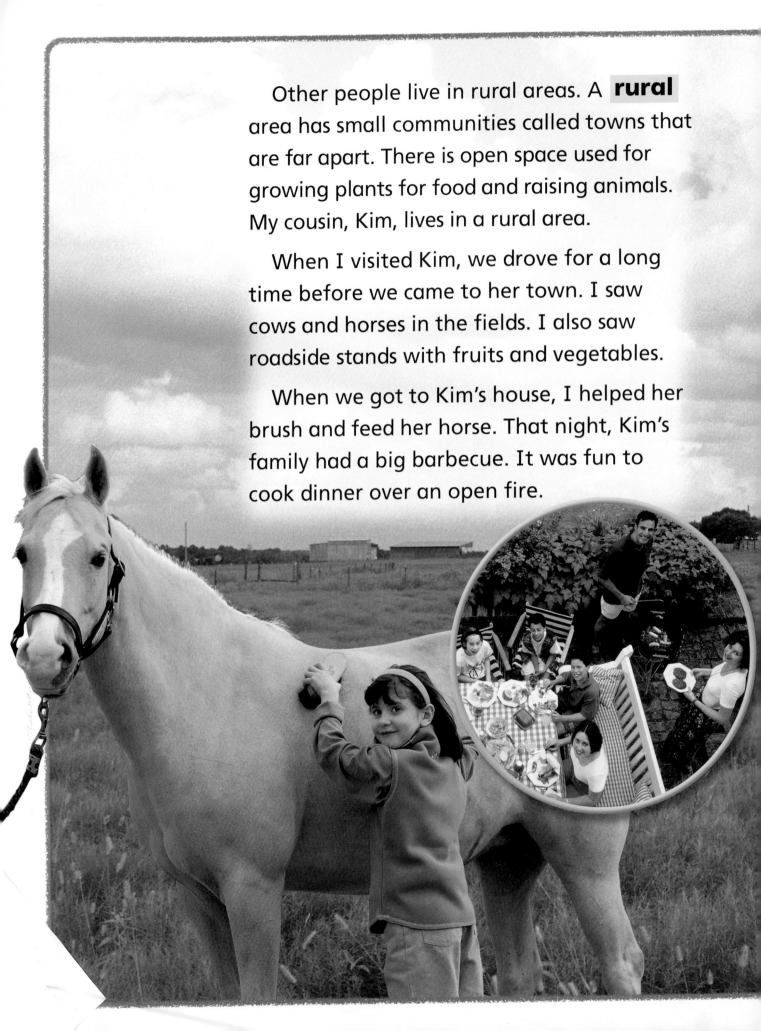

Other people live in rural areas. A **rural** area has small communities called towns that are far apart. There is open space used for growing plants for food and raising animals. My cousin, Kim, lives in a rural area.

When I visited Kim, we drove for a long time before we came to her town. I saw cows and horses in the fields. I also saw roadside stands with fruits and vegetables.

When we got to Kim's house, I helped her brush and feed her horse. That night, Kim's family had a big barbecue. It was fun to cook dinner over an open fire.

There is something I like about each of these places. If you could live in one of these communities, which one would you choose? Why?

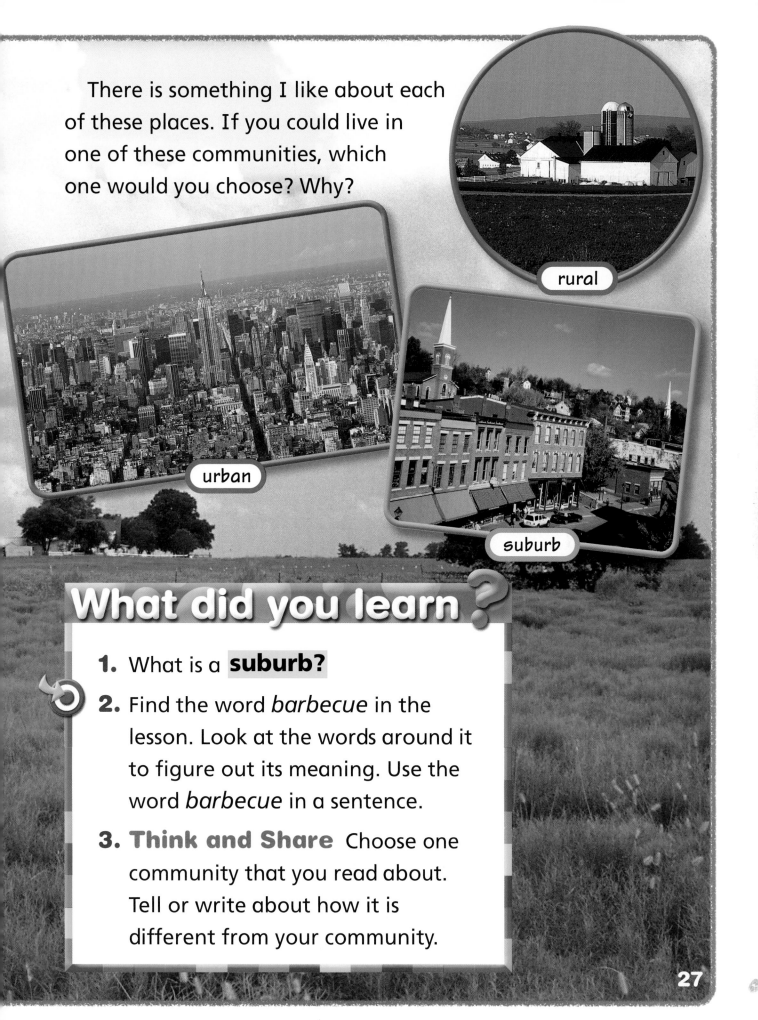

rural

urban

suburb

What did you learn ?

1. What is a **suburb**?

2. Find the word *barbecue* in the lesson. Look at the words around it to figure out its meaning. Use the word *barbecue* in a sentence.

3. **Think and Share** Choose one community that you read about. Tell or write about how it is different from your community.

Meet
Rosalynn Carter

1927–
Former First Lady and Humanitarian

Rosalynn Carter works to help people in communities everywhere. She has received the Presidential Medal of Freedom for her work. This is the highest honor a civilian in the United States can receive.

28

After her father died, young Rosalynn helped her mother by doing household chores and looking after her brothers and sister. She also worked hard in school and made very good grades.

When she was older, Rosalynn married Jimmy Carter. Later, Jimmy Carter was elected the governor of Georgia and then the President of the United States. During this time, Rosalynn Carter worked hard to help people. She worked on programs to aid mental health care, elderly people, and the community.

Today, Rosalynn Carter is still involved in helping people in the community, the country, and around the world. She has been given many honors for her work.

Rosalynn Carter was born in Plains, Georgia.

Rosalynn Carter

Rosalynn and Jimmy Carter

Think and Share

What has Rosalynn Carter done to help people?

For more information, go online to *Meet the People* at **www.sfsocialstudies.com.**

Our State and Our Country

Our class is learning about the fifty states that make up our country. Our country is called the United States of America. I did a report on Georgia where Rosalynn Carter was born. In my report, I included symbols, or pictures that stand for this state.

Georgia

Georgia has many symbols.

This bird stands for Georgia.

This flower does too.

Georgia's flag is red,

white, gold, and blue.

Look at Georgia's border. A border is a line that divides one state or country from another. Trace the border around Georgia. What are the five states that share its border?

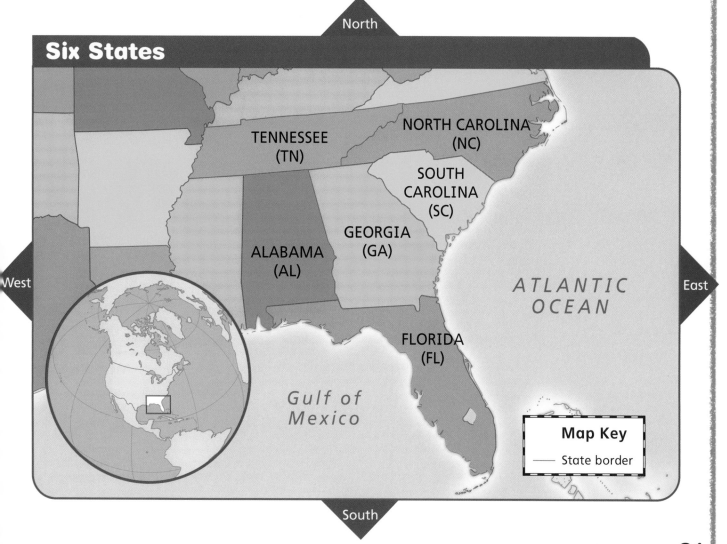

Six States

North

TENNESSEE
(TN)

NORTH CAROLINA
(NC)

SOUTH
CAROLINA
(SC)

GEORGIA
(GA)

ALABAMA
(AL)

ATLANTIC
OCEAN

West

East

FLORIDA
(FL)

Gulf of
Mexico

Map Key

— State border

South

Our country has fifty states. Find your state on this map. What are the states that share a border with your state?

Canada and Mexico are two countries that share borders with the United States. Trace the border that the United States shares with our neighbor to the south, Mexico. Trace the border that the United States shares with Canada, our neighbor to the north.

The United States

North

West

East

South

ARCTIC OCEAN

CANADA

ALASKA

PACIFIC OCEAN

CANADA

WASHINGTON

OREGON

IDAHO

MONTANA

NORTH DAKOTA

SOUTH DAKOTA

WYOMING

NEVADA

UTAH

CALIFORNIA

COLORADO

ARIZONA

NEW MEXICO

MINNESOTA

WISCONSIN

MICHIGAN

IOWA

NEBRASKA

KANSAS

MISSOURI

ILLINOIS

INDIANA

OHIO

KENTUCKY

TENNESSEE

OKLAHOMA

ARKANSAS

TEXAS

MISSISSIPPI

ALABAMA

LOUISIANA

NEW HAMPSHIRE

VERMONT

MAINE

MASSACHUSETTS

RHODE ISLAND

CONNECTICUT

NEW YORK

PENNSYLVANIA

NEW JERSEY

DELAWARE

MARYLAND

WEST VIRGINIA

VIRGINIA

Washington, D.C.

NORTH CAROLINA

SOUTH CAROLINA

GEORGIA

FLORIDA

ATLANTIC OCEAN

PACIFIC OCEAN

HAWAII

PACIFIC OCEAN

MEXICO

Gulf of Mexico

Map Key

⊛ National capital

— State border

— Country border

32

In my report, I learned that Atlanta is the capital of Georgia. A **capital** is a city where the leaders of a state work. What is the name of your state's capital?

Our country has a capital too. It is Washington, D.C. This is the home of the President, who is our country's leader. Washington, D.C., is the place where people chosen from each state vote to make our country's laws.

Washington, D.C.

What did you learn ?

1. What two countries share a border with the United States?

2. Where is our country's **capital** located?

3. **Think and Share** Draw an outline map of your state. Include its capital. Put a title on the map. Around the map, draw symbols that stand for your state.

Meet Benjamin Banneker

1731–1806
Surveyor and Inventor

Benjamin Banneker lived during the time when George Washington was President. He helped President Washington plan a new capital city for our nation.

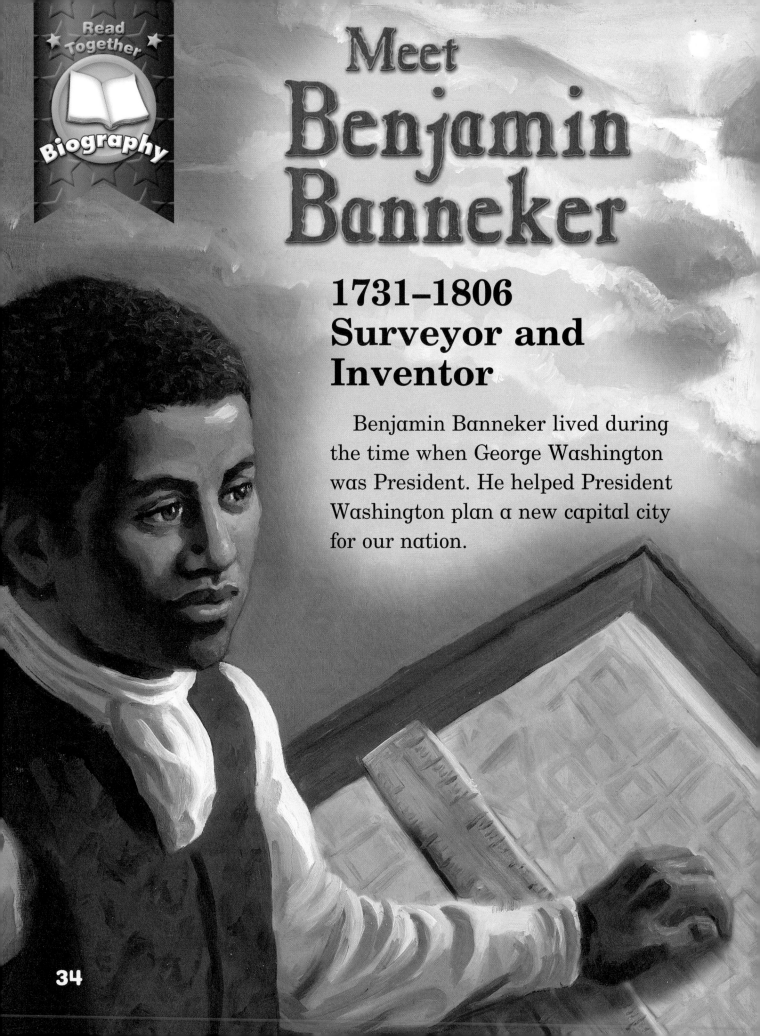

Benjamin Banneker grew up on a farm in Maryland. His grandmother taught him to read. Benjamin also studied math. He attended school until he was old enough to spend his days working on the farm.

As a young man, Benjamin Banneker had never seen a clock. He was shown a pocket watch. He carefully looked at the watch. Then he built a wooden clock that kept the correct time for many years.

President Washington wanted to build a new capital city for our nation. The city was to be named Washington, District of Columbia. Many people worked together to build this new city. Benjamin Banneker was part of a team of surveyors. Surveyors measure an area of land. Benjamin Banneker helped measure the land for Washington, D.C.

Benjamin Banneker returned to the farm. He wrote an almanac, or booklike calendar, that included information about the sun, moon, and stars.

Benjamin Banneker was born near Baltimore, Maryland.

Benjamin Banneker, 1795

Think and Share

How did Benjamin Banneker help build the capital city of our nation, Washington, D.C.?

For more information, go online to *Meet the People* at **www.sfsocialstudies.com**.

Lesson 5

Our Country Is Part of Our World

Where do you live? There are many ways to answer the question. Look at my picture to see how I answered the question.

How would you answer the question?

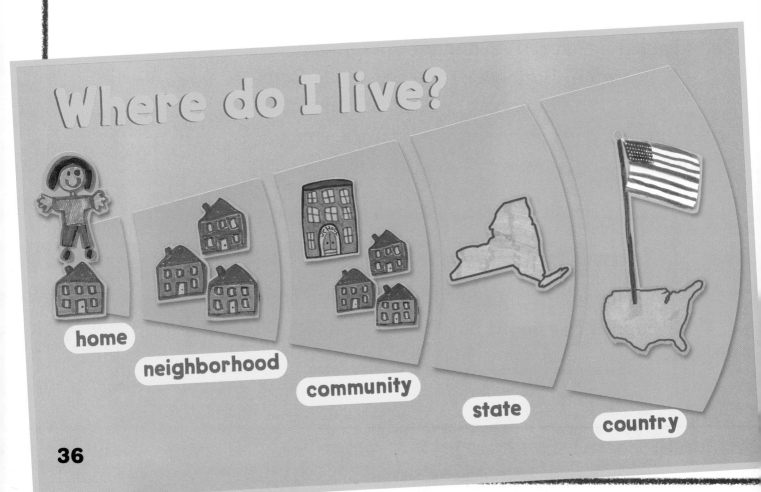

Where do I live?

home

neighborhood

community

state

country

There are more ways I can tell about where I live. Remember when we looked at borders that the United States shares with Canada and Mexico? These three countries are part of a continent, or large body of land, called North America.

A globe is a model of Earth. Look on this globe to find North America. What are the names of the oceans, or large bodies of salt water, around North America?

Where *do* I live? I live on a continent called North America.

This is a map of the world. You can see continents and oceans on this map. You can also see the equator. The equator is a line found on a map of the world that divides the world in half.

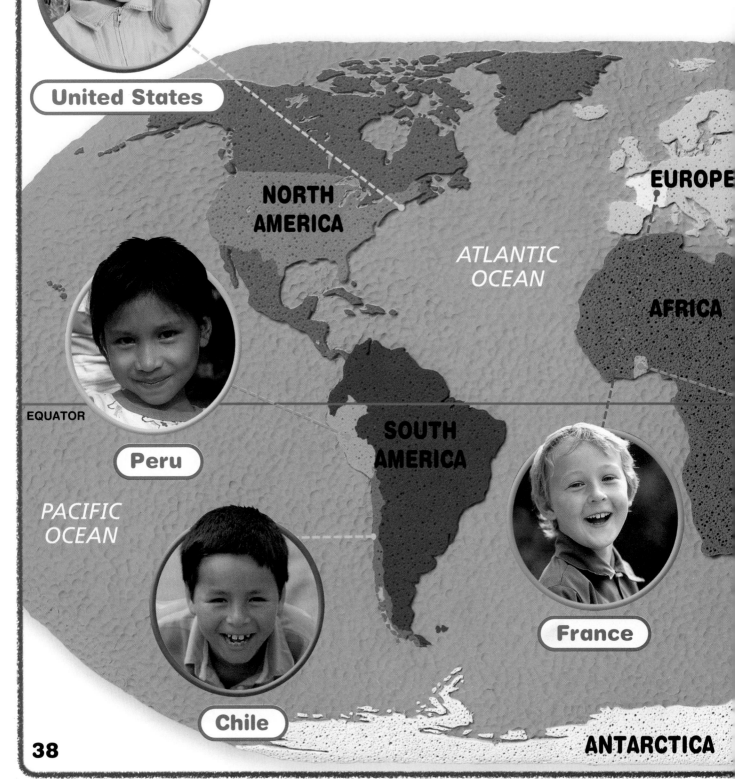

United States

NORTH AMERICA

EUROPE

ATLANTIC OCEAN

AFRICA

EQUATOR

Peru

SOUTH AMERICA

PACIFIC OCEAN

France

Chile

ANTARCTICA

Meet some children from different countries around the world. What can you tell about where each child lives?

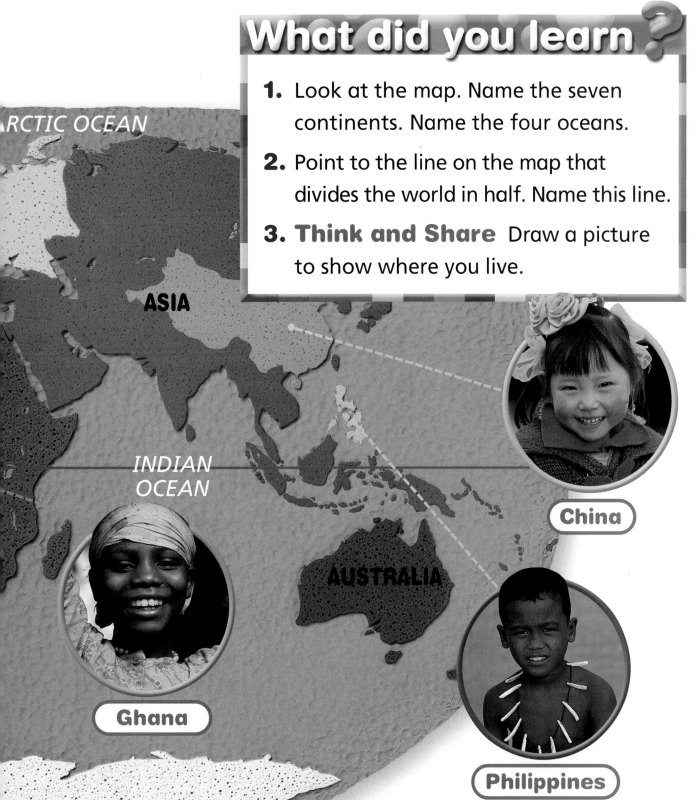

ARCTIC OCEAN

ASIA

INDIAN OCEAN

AUSTRALIA

China

Ghana

Philippines

What did you learn?

1. Look at the map. Name the seven continents. Name the four oceans.

2. Point to the line on the map that divides the world in half. Name this line.

3. **Think and Share** Draw a picture to show where you live.

Children of the World

Oscar
Bolivia

Carlitos
Argentina

Mohammed
Egypt

Tadesse
Ethiopia

Children all around the world are busy doing the same things. They love to play games and they enjoy going to school. They wish for peace. They think that adults should take good care of the Earth. How else do you think these children are like each other? How else do you think they are like you?

NORTH AMERICA

SOUTH AMERICA

Bolivia

Argentina

Aseye
Ghana

Esta
Tanzania

Sarala
India

Yong-Koo and Ji-Koo
South Korea

Ngawaiata
New Zealand

Rachel
France

Yannis
Greece

Monika
Hungary

Bogna
Poland

Daisuke
Japan

Erdene
Mongolia

Thi Liên
Vietnam

Edgar
Philippines

Subaedah
Indonesia

ASIA

EUROPE

Poland

France   Hungary

Greece

Egypt

AFRICA

Ghana

Ethiopia

Tanzania

Mongolia

Japan

South
Korea

India

Vietnam

Philippines

Indonesia

AUSTRALIA

New Zealand

In the Country, In the City

by Charles Wood

Mom walks.
Baby talks.
Frogs croak.
Chimneys smoke.
Cows moo.
Birds coo.
Leaves rustle.
Horses bustle.
Flowers grow.
Streams flow.

People shop.
Cars stop.
Bikers coast.
Chestnuts roast.
Trains zoom by.
Babies cry.
Buses go.
Signs glow.
Runners run.

We have fun!

Vocabulary Review

Tell which word completes each sentence.

1. You make a choice when you _____.

2. A rule that everyone must follow is called a _____.

3. Many neighborhoods make up a _____.

4. The story of people and places from the past is _____.

5. A community located near a city is a _____.

★ ★ ★ ★ ★ ★ ★ ★

TEST PREP Which word completes each sentence?

1. A city is called an _____ area.

   a. rural   **b.** community

   c. urban   **d.** suburb

2. A lot of open space and towns that are far apart is called a _____ area.

   a. rural   **b.** community

   c. urban   **d.** capital

Skills Review

 **Use Context Clues**

Read the following passage.

A capital is a city where leaders of a state make laws and work. Leaders from North Carolina work in the capital city of Raleigh.

Tell the meaning of *capital*. If you don't know what the word means, look at the words around it to help you find its meaning.

Solve a Problem

Think of a problem that you want to solve. Tell or write about it, using this six-step plan:

1. Name the problem.

2. Find out more about the problem.

3. List ways to solve the problem.

4. Talk about the best way to solve the problem.

5. Solve the problem.

6. How well is the problem solved?

Read a Map

This map shows a courthouse, a library, and other buildings that you might have in your community. Use the map key and direction arrows to help you answer these questions.

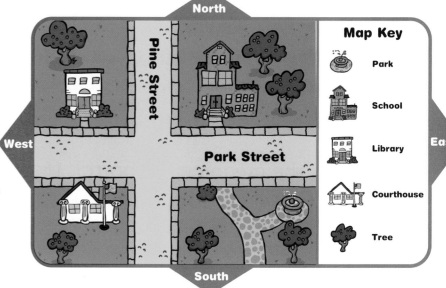

1. What direction would you go if you were walking from the library to the courthouse?

2. What street is in front of the 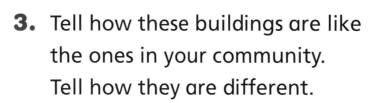 ?

3. Tell how these buildings are like the ones in your community. Tell how they are different.

Skills On Your Own

Draw your own map of a community. Include a map key with symbols that stand for a library, a post office, a hospital, a courthouse, and other buildings.

What did you learn?

1. Describe two neighborhoods in your community.

2. Why are laws important?

3. How are urban, suburban, and rural communities alike? How are they different?

4. **Write and Share** Tell or write about where you live. Tell something about your community, state, and country.

Test Talk

Look for key words in the question.

Read About Where You Live

Look for books like these in the library.

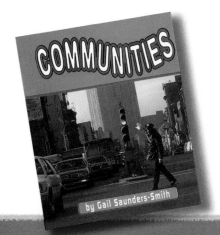

COMMUNITIES

by Gail Saunders-Smith

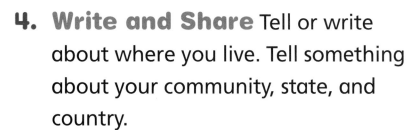

ANN MORRIS
HOUSES AND HOMES
PHOTOGRAPHS BY KEN HEYMAN

City Green
DyAnne DiSalvo-Ryan

Discovery
CHANNEL
SCHOOL

UNIT
1 Project

Travel Channel

Travel reporters share their thoughts about places to visit.

1 Choose a place to visit that is urban, suburban, or rural.

2 Make a travel booklet about the place you chose. Draw pictures of what a visitor might see or do there.

3 Write words to describe your pictures. Tell what makes your place rural, urban, or suburban.

4 Present your booklet to the class. Tell why people might like to go to your place.

Internet Activity

Go to www.sfsocialstudies.com/activities to learn more about communities.

48

Show You Care

by Emily Sasaki

Sung to the tune of
"Yankee Doodle"

You may live upon the plains
Or near a hill or lake.
Show you care about the Earth.
There are simple steps to take!
Care for land and wildlife too.
Let's take care of our nation.
Keep our air and water clean
And practice conservation!

51

geography

landform

ancestor

producer

Soil

Apple Juice

Great Grandma's Pies

Pumpkins

Welcome To
Reyes Family Farm
Since 1898

Our Map

consumer

natural resource

crop

conservation

Sara Helps Plants Grow

Target Skill

Cause and Effect

Hi, I'm Sara. My family and I live on a farm in South Carolina. We grow apples. In school, I am learning about growing other fruits and vegetables. In my classroom, I am in charge of watering the plants. When I water the plants, they grow.

A **cause** is what makes something happen. An **effect** is what happens. One cause is watering a plant. The effect is that a plant will grow.

cause

effect

Try it!

Write the words **cause** and **effect**. Ask the teacher to switch off the lights. What caused the lights to go off? Write this under **cause.** What happened when the lights were switched off? Write this under **effect.**

SUNFLOWER
Cutting Gold

SUNFLOWER
Evening Sun

Interview with a Geographer

Sara   What does a geographer do?

Mrs. Bond   I study geography. **Geography** is the study of Earth and the ways people use it.

Sara   What else does a geographer do?

Mrs. Bond   I study the Earth's surface. The surface of the Earth has many different shapes. Each kind of shape is a **landform.** For example, a hill is a landform. A hill is a high place on the Earth's surface.

mountain

Mrs. Bond

A mountain is a landform. A mountain is the highest kind of land.

plain

Mrs. Bond

This is a plain. A plain is a large, mostly flat, area of land. Many farms are found on plains.

valley

Mrs. Bond

This is a valley, or a low area of land. A valley is usually found between mountains or hills.

island

Sara

Can you tell me about land that is near water?

Mrs. Bond

An island is land that is surrounded by water.

Mrs. Bond

A peninsula is land that is almost surrounded by water.

peninsula

Sara

In school, we learned that an ocean is a huge body of salt water.

ocean

Mrs. Bond

That's right! Bodies of water also have different sizes and shapes. A river is a stream of fresh water. Rivers usually flow toward a lake or an ocean.

river

Mrs. Bond

This is a lake. It is a large body of water surrounded by land.

Sara

Thank you for teaching me about geography.

lake

What did you learn?

1. What is **geography?**

2. Name a **landform** and a body of water. Draw a picture of each.

3. **Think and Share** It is cold at the top of the mountain so the snow does not melt. Tell the **cause** and the **effect.**

Landforms and Water on a Map

This is a map of South Carolina. This map will help Sara find different types of land and water in the state where she lives.

North

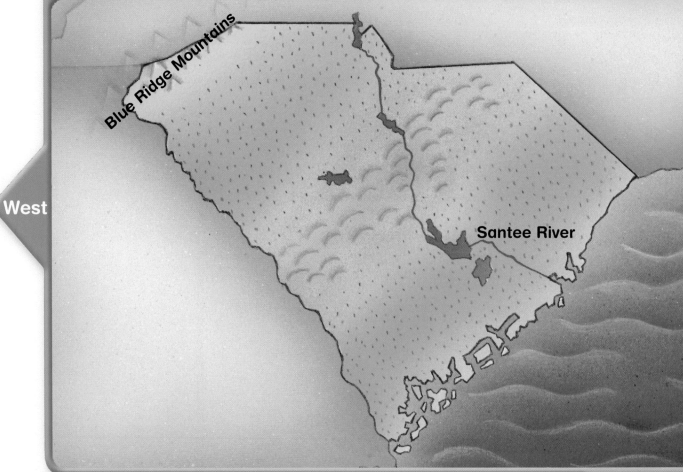

South Carolina

Blue Ridge Mountains

Santee River

West

South

For more information, go online to the *Atlas* at **www.sfsocialstudies.com.**

Look at the map key. Find the colors and symbols that stand for landforms and bodies of water.

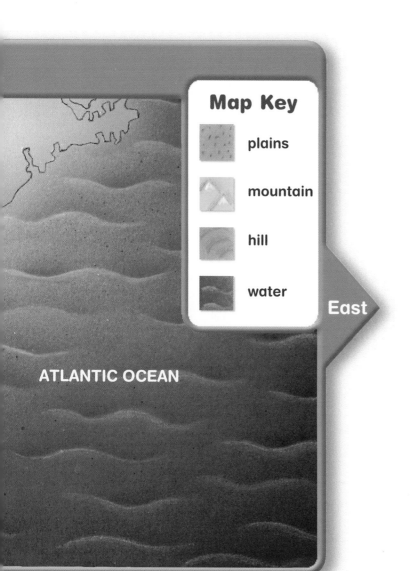

Map Key

plains

mountain

hill

water

East

ATLANTIC OCEAN

Try it!

1. Find the symbol for mountain. What mountain range do you see on the map?

2. Into what body of water does the Santee River flow?

3. **On Your Own** Make your own land and water map. Include colors and symbols for a mountain, hill, lake, and river.

Where People Live

Our class has pen pals who live in three different places. Come and meet our new friends.

Tucson, Arizona

Juan

Hi!

I live in Tucson, Arizona. My city is near a hot and dry desert.

Last week, my class took a field trip to a really great museum about the desert. Did you know that many animals and plants live in the desert?

Rabbits, snakes, and even coyotes live here. The cactuses grow in many shapes and sizes. A cactus can store water and live through months of dry weather.

What kind of plants and animals live around you?

Write back soon.

Juan

P.S. I like bike riding, baseball, and swimming. What do you like to do?

Sonoran Desert

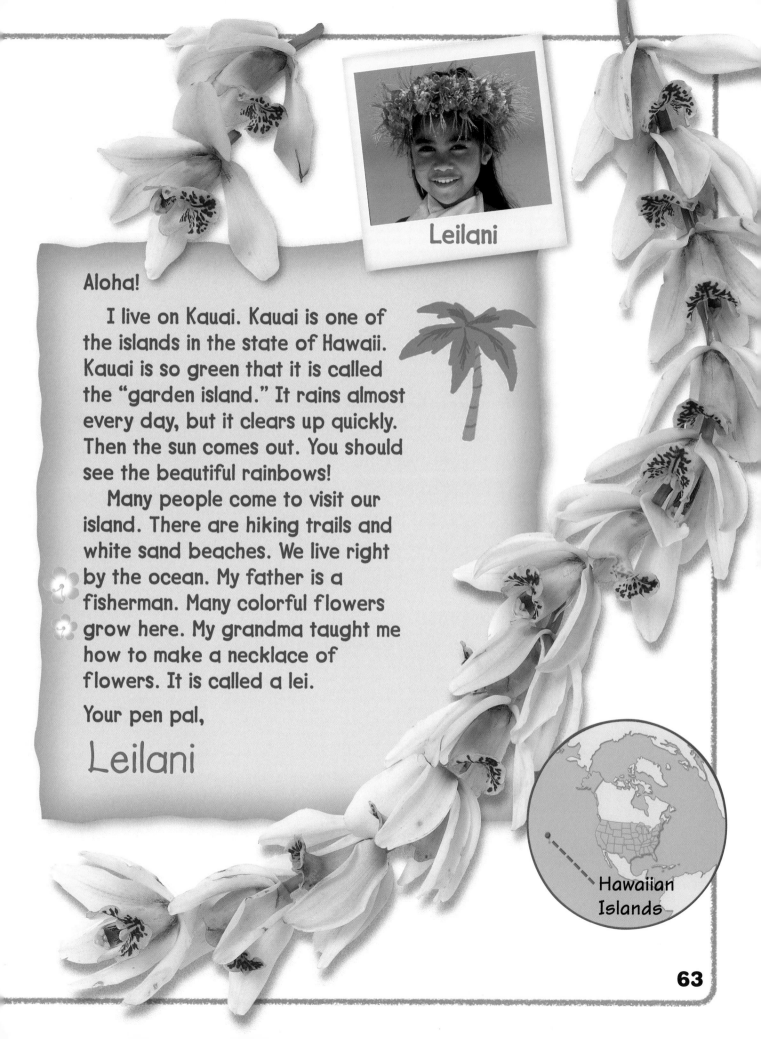

Leilani

Aloha!

I live on Kauai. Kauai is one of the islands in the state of Hawaii. Kauai is so green that it is called the "garden island." It rains almost every day, but it clears up quickly. Then the sun comes out. You should see the beautiful rainbows!

Many people come to visit our island. There are hiking trails and white sand beaches. We live right by the ocean. My father is a fisherman. Many colorful flowers grow here. My grandma taught me how to make a necklace of flowers. It is called a lei.

Your pen pal,

Leilani

Hawaiian Islands

Statesboro, Georgia

Matt

Hello!

I live on a farm near Statesboro, Georgia. My family grows corn and soybeans. We also raise hogs. Living on a farm is quieter than living in a town. There isn't much traffic. The houses are farther apart.

We just came back from the Georgia State Fair. I had a great time. My big brother's pig won a blue ribbon.

Write back soon.

Matt

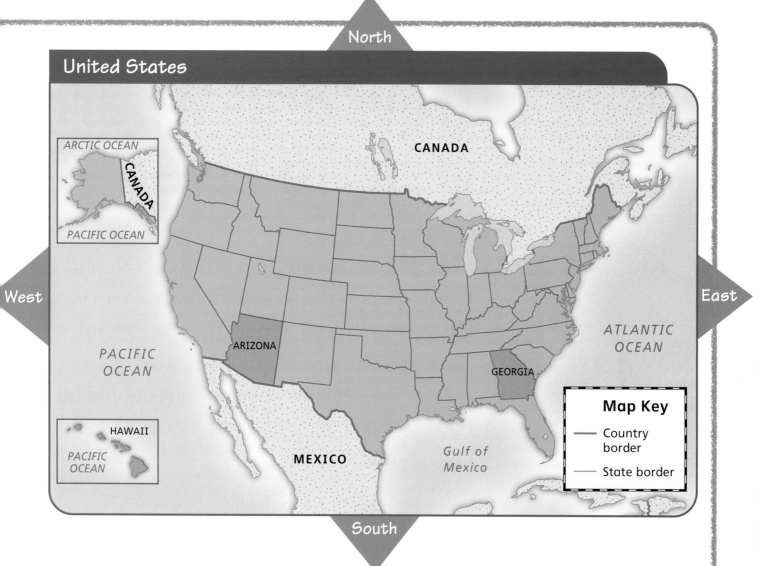

United States

North

West

East

South

ARCTIC OCEAN

CANADA

PACIFIC OCEAN

CANADA

ATLANTIC OCEAN

PACIFIC OCEAN

ARIZONA

GEORGIA

HAWAII

PACIFIC OCEAN

MEXICO

Gulf of Mexico

Map Key
— Country border
— State border

Look at the map. Find Arizona, Georgia, and Hawaii.

What did you learn?

1. Which of the three states in this lesson shares a border with Mexico?

2. Which state is a group of islands in the Pacific Ocean?

3. **Think and Share** Compare the place you live with one of the communities you read about in the pen pal letters.

How and Where People Lived

Some Native Americans made canoes, or narrow boats, to travel on the rivers.

Native Americans, also known as American Indians, were the first people to live in what is now the United States. They used land, water, plants, and animals to meet their needs. A need is something that people must have to live. Food, clothing, and a place to live are needs.

Native Americans lived in areas with different climates. Climate is the kind of weather a place usually has. Native Americans built homes to suit the climate. They used things found in nature to make their homes.

Many groups of Native Americans lived in an area called the Great Plains. These Native Americans were called Plains Indians. Some Plains Indians were farmers. They planned their lives around the changing seasons. Spring was the time to plant. Fall was the time to harvest.

Painted animal skin

Sometimes terrible storms and floods happened on the plains. How would these very bad weather conditions have affected the crops? How might bad weather conditions affect the activities of farmers today?

Many Plains Indians hunted animals for food. They used animal skins to keep warm. Some lived in a kind of tent called a tepee.

Today life has changed for many Native Americans. Some are still farmers while others have jobs in towns or cities.

Hands-on History

Draw and label pictures of things Native Americans might have used to meet their needs. Tell or write about some things you use to meet your needs.

From My Orchard to You

A long time ago, my great-grandfather had a small apple orchard. My great-grandfather is my ancestor. An **ancestor** is a person in our family who lived before we were born. This picture shows some of my ancestors.

The people in my family are producers of apples. A **producer** is someone who makes or grows something. We use and change the land to grow our tasty apples. Here's what we do to get the apples from the orchard to you!

Workers prune, or cut, the branches of the trees. This lets more sunlight reach the trees so the apples ripen. Pruning also makes it easier to pick the apples.

winter

We clear some of the land to make room for new trees to be planted. We cut tall grass to keep away harmful insects. Sometimes we spray to protect the trees and fruit from insects.

spring

summer

We irrigate if we don't get enough rain. Irrigate means to bring water to the land. Irrigation can be done by using ditches or sprinkling. When we irrigate the land, the crops grow well. Irrigation is the **cause.** What is the **effect?**

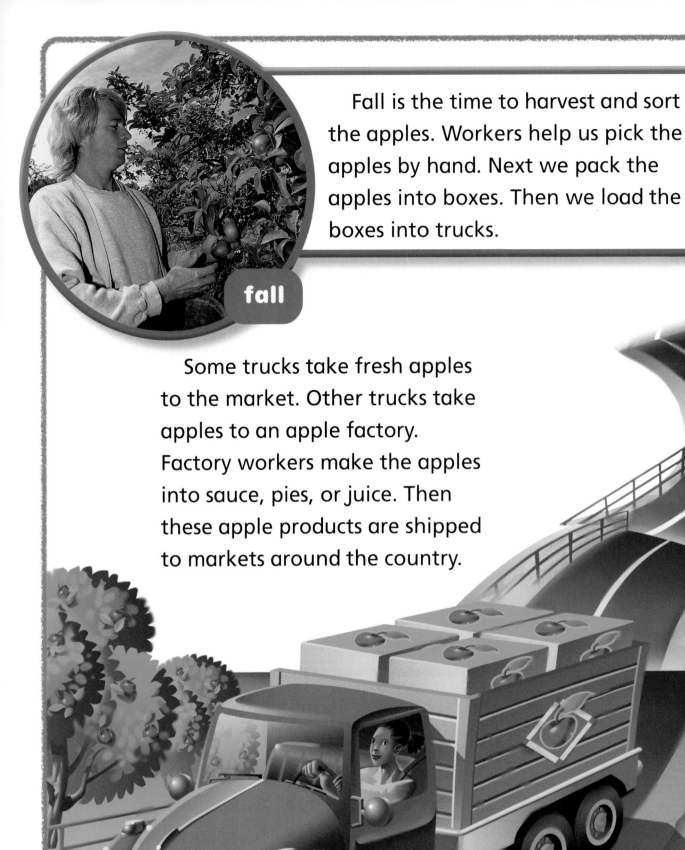

Fall is the time to harvest and sort the apples. Workers help us pick the apples by hand. Next we pack the apples into boxes. Then we load the boxes into trucks.

fall

Some trucks take fresh apples to the market. Other trucks take apples to an apple factory. Factory workers make the apples into sauce, pies, or juice. Then these apple products are shipped to markets around the country.

At the market, workers put the apples and apple products on shelves for consumers just like you. A **consumer** is someone who buys and uses goods. Goods are things that people make or grow. What other goods do consumers buy at the market?

What did you learn?

1. What is the difference between **producers** and **consumers?**

2. How does Sara's family use or change the land? How do people in your community use or change the land?

3. **Think and Share** Draw two pictures showing yourself as a producer and as a consumer. Tell about each picture.

Growing Crops

Farmers around the world grow fruits and vegetables all year long. Fresh fruits and vegetables are delivered to your market almost every day. What are your favorite fruits and vegetables?

Many people like to pick their own raspberries.

Pineapples grow up from the ground on short stems.

Grapes grow on a vine. They are often picked by hand.

This plow turns the soil over. Then farmers can plant seeds.

Some peas are still picked from the vine by hand.

These plants are being grown without soil. Their roots are in a liquid that has food to help them grow.

Bananas do not grow on trees. They grow in bunches on tall banana plants.

The part of the potato plant that we eat grows underground.

This is called a greenhouse. Plants can be grown in a greenhouse all year long.

Pears are often grown in orchards such as this one.

Biography

Meet Cesar Chavez

1927–1993
Organizer and Leader

Cesar Chavez was a strong leader. He made life better for farm workers. The group he organized continues to help farm workers.

As a child, Cesar Chavez lived on a small farm in Arizona. When Cesar was ten, his family had to give up their farm. The Chavez family became migrant farm workers. They followed the harvest in California. They picked crops that other farmers had grown. Cesar attended more than thirty different schools as the family moved from place to place.

Cesar Chavez was born near Yuma, Arizona.

After eighth-grade graduation, Cesar ended his education. He began working full-time in the fields. Life for Cesar, and other migrant workers, was very hard. They worked long hours for low pay. They often lived in their cars or trucks.

Cesar Chavez wanted to make life better for farm workers. He began to teach Mexican farm workers to read and write. He helped them become citizens so they could vote. Cesar organized the farm workers into a group called a *union*. He became their leader. He helped farm workers get fair pay and better working conditions.

Cesar Chavez School in San Francisco, CA

Think and Share

How did Cesar Chavez help farm workers?

 For more information, go online to *Meet the People* at **www.sfsocialstudies.com.**

Our Earth's Resources

A **natural resource** is a useful material that comes from the Earth. All living things depend on natural resources. Air, water, sun, forests, and soil are natural resources.

All of these things come from trees.

Farmers use natural resources to raise animals such as sheep. Sheep give us wool. During the winter, a sheep's coat of wool grows. When springtime comes, the sheep's wool gets cut. Luckily, it grows back, just like our hair!

Shearing sheep for wool

All of these things are made from sheep's wool.

Farmers also use natural resources to raise crops. A **crop** is a kind of plant grown by people for food and other uses. Wheat is one kind of crop that is grown on the Great Plains. Most wheat is grown for food.

Wheat

Look at my kitchen table. The foods you see are made from wheat.

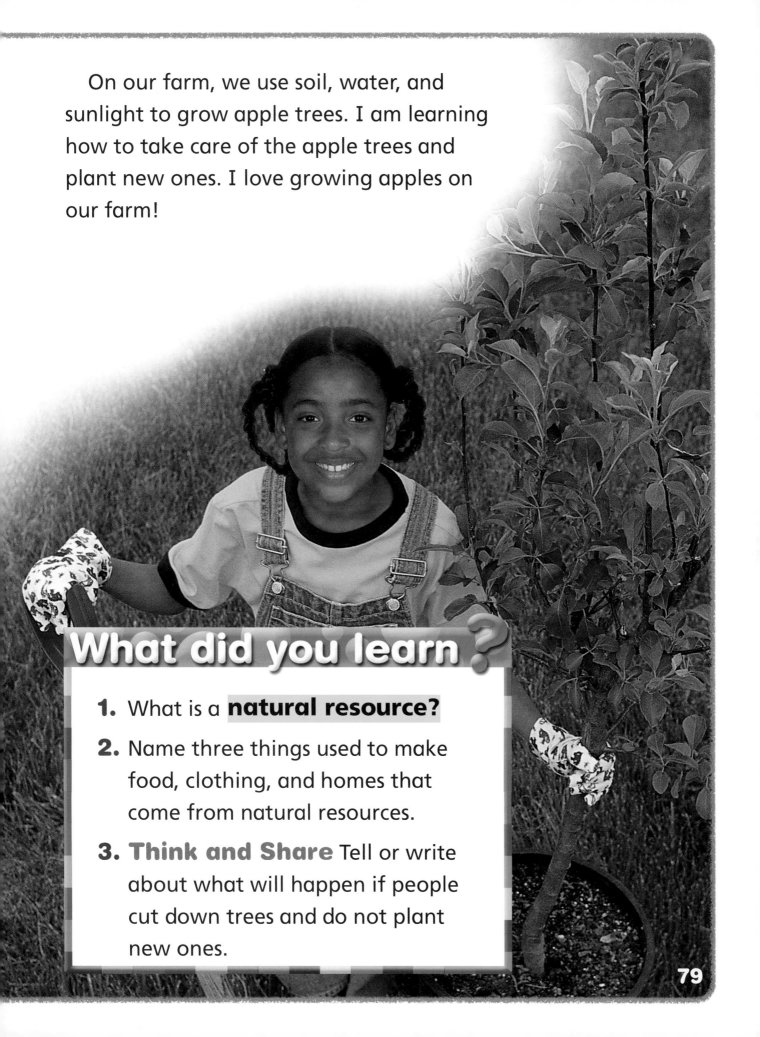

On our farm, we use soil, water, and sunlight to grow apple trees. I am learning how to take care of the apple trees and plant new ones. I love growing apples on our farm!

What did you learn?

1. What is a **natural resource?**

2. Name three things used to make food, clothing, and homes that come from natural resources.

3. **Think and Share** Tell or write about what will happen if people cut down trees and do not plant new ones.

Read a Bar Graph

Sara's class made a bar graph of different kinds of fruit. A **bar graph** helps you compare groups. Look at the bar graph.

Our Favorite Fruit

	1	2	3	4	5	6	7	8	9
bananas									
oranges									
apples									
strawberries									

The title of the graph is "Our Favorite Fruit." On the side of the bar graph, find the name of each fruit. What kinds of fruit does the class like? The bottom of the bar graph shows the number of children. Look at the bar next to the oranges. How many children picked oranges?

Try it!

1. What is the favorite fruit in Sara's class?

2. Name the two fruits that got the same number of votes.

3. **On Your Own** Make a **bar graph** of other foods that you like. Ask classmates to vote on which food they like the best.

Caring for Our Resources

Yellowstone National Park, Wyoming

Last summer, I visited Yellowstone National Park in Wyoming. Yellowstone is the oldest national park in the United States. In national parks, conservation is very important. **Conservation** is the care and protection of land, water, plants, and animals. In the park, people are not allowed to cut down trees, litter, or take away any of the plants or animals.

Bison herd in Yellowstone National Park

When I grow up, I hope to become a park ranger. It would be my job to protect the plants and animals. I would help workers plant new trees.

While visiting Yellowstone, I was in the Junior Ranger program. We learned about important park rules. One rule is to stay on the trails. We do this so we do not get lost. We also do this so we do not step on plants or disturb the animals. The park ranger reminds us not to tease or feed the animals.

Yellowstone Park Ranger

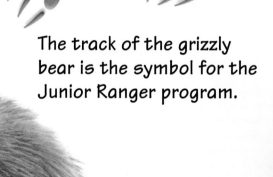

The track of the grizzly bear is the symbol for the Junior Ranger program.

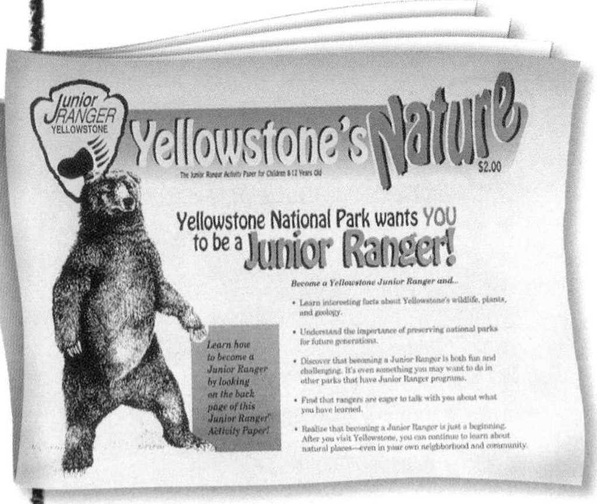

I got a Junior Ranger newspaper on my first day at the park. In my newspaper, I drew the route my family took through Yellowstone Park. In my journal, I wrote about favorite things I saw.

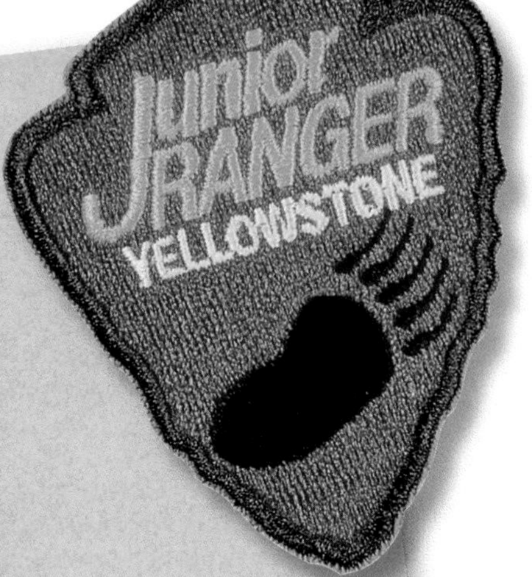

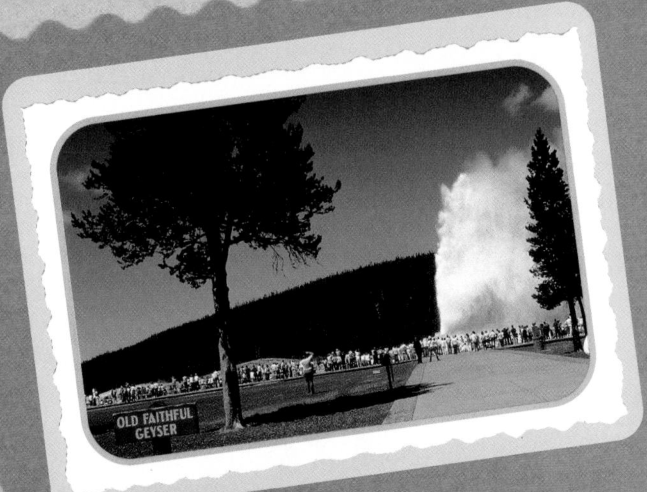

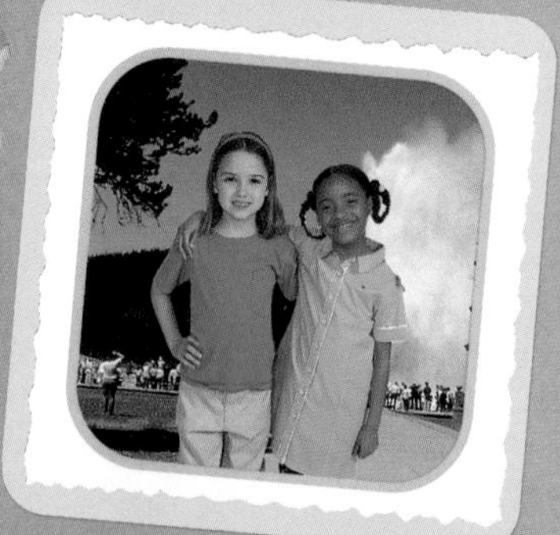

OLD FAITHFUL GEYSER

Yellowstone has more than 300 geysers. Geysers are underground springs that throw hot water and steam into the air. I've never seen anything like them before!

7

I told my class about being a Junior Ranger. We talked about things we can do to help protect and conserve the park in our neighborhood.

Smell the flowers, but don't pick them!

Please don't litter.

Please stay on the trails.

Please don't feed or tease the animals.

What did you learn?

1. Why is it important to learn about **conservation?**

2. What is the job of a park ranger?

3. **Think and Share** Make a poster showing ways you can help conserve the resources in your community.

Meet Rachel Carson

1907–1964

Writer and Biologist

Rachel Louise Carson had a lifelong love of nature. She wrote about our resources and how to conserve them.

As a child, Rachel loved books. When she was ten, she published her first story. Rachel's mother encouraged her to write and introduced her to nature.

When she grew older, Rachel could not decide whether she wanted to become a writer or a biologist. One of her teachers convinced Rachel that she could be both.

As a biologist and writer, Rachel Carson dedicated her life to conserving the Earth's resources. She was especially interested in protecting birds, fish, and other wildlife. She wrote newspaper articles and books to help this cause. Rachel Carson also worked to have laws passed to protect our resources.

Rachel Carson wrote books to teach people about the beauty of the Earth. Two of her books, *The Sea Around Us* and *Silent Spring,* were bestsellers. One article she wrote was turned into a book for parents. It is called *The Sense of Wonder.*

Rachel Carson was born in Springdale, Pennsylvania.

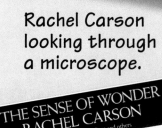

Rachel Carson looking through a microscope.

THE SENSE OF WONDER
RACHEL CARSON
Photographs by Charles Pratt and others

Words and pictures to help you keep alive your child's inborn sense of wonder and renew your own delight in the mysteries of earth, sea and sky

The best-selling environmental classic

Think and Share

Tell how Rachel Carson helped protect the Earth's resources.

 For more information, go online to *Meet the People* at **www.sfsocialstudies.com.**

The Earth Angels

The Earth Angels of the Guardian Angel Settlement are located in St. Louis, Missouri.

The Earth Angels is a group of children from St. Louis, Missouri. They are responsible for many projects that help protect the Earth's resources.

In 1999, the Earth Angels won the President's Environmental Youth Award. They won for building special nesting boxes for birds. These nesting boxes protected birds and gave them a place to live. The Earth Angels built 100 nesting boxes. Most were hung at the children's homes and in nearby parks.

BUILDING CITIZENSHIP
Caring
Respect
★ Responsibility
Fairness
Honesty
Courage

The Earth Angels also have made wildlife habitats in the city. Habitats are places where plants and animals live. The habitats include a prairie garden and butterfly gardens.

The Earth Angels raise money to pay for their projects. They raise money through recycling. They also sell Earth Angel buttons.

The Earth Angels rescue animals and find homes for them. They plant trees in parks. These children are always thinking of new ways to take responsibility for helping the world around them.

Planting a butterfly garden

★ Responsibility in Action ★

How do the Earth Angels show they are responsible citizens in their community? How can you be a responsible citizen in your community?

89

America, the Beautiful
by Katharine Lee Bates

O beautiful for spacious skies,
For amber waves of grain,
For purple mountain majesties
Above the fruited plain!
America! America!
God shed His grace on thee
And crown thy good with brotherhood
From sea to shining sea.

Vocabulary Review

natural resource

landform

geography

conservation

ancestor

Find the correct meaning for each word.

1. a shape on the surface of the Earth

2. the study of the Earth and the ways people use it

3. something useful that comes from the Earth

4. a person in our family who lived before we were born

5. the care and protection of land, water, plants, and animals

★ ★ ★ ★ ★ ★ ★ ★

TEST PREP   Which word completes each sentence?

1. Someone who buys and uses goods is called a _____.
   a. producer   **b.** consumer
   c. geography   **d.** conservation

Test Talk

Find key words in the text.

2. Someone who makes or grows something is called a _____.
   a. producer   **b.** consumer
   c. crop   **d.** conservation

Skills Review

⊙ Cause and Effect

Tell the **cause** and **effect** in each sentence.

1. We irrigated, so the corn grew tall.

2. I feel warm because I am wearing a wool sweater.

Landforms and Water on a Map

1. The Rio Grande is part of the border between what two countries?

2. What mountains do you see west of the Mississippi River?

3. What bodies of water do you see on the map between Canada and the United States?

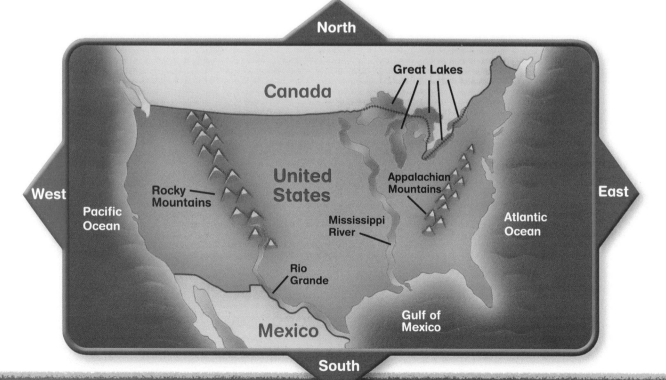

Skills Review
Read a Bar Graph

Sara's class voted for their favorite foods made from apples. Use the bar graph to answer the questions.

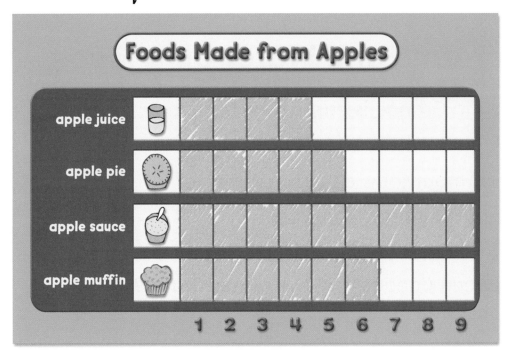

1. Which food do most of the children like best?

2. How many children picked apple muffins?

3. Which food was picked the fewest times?

Skills On Your Own

Make a bar graph of foods made from wheat, such as bread, pasta, and crackers. Write a name for your graph. Ask some friends to vote on the food they like the best.

What did you learn?

1. Draw and label three landforms.

2. Identify ways people depend on natural resources to meet their needs.

3. What are two ways of irrigating land?

4. **Write and Share** Tell or write about what could happen if we do not take care of our resources.

Read About Our Earth and Its Resources

Look for books like these in the library.

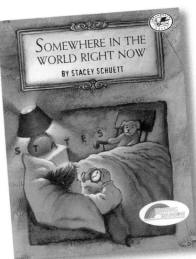

UNIT 2 Project

Guess My Place

On this game show, you will try to guess a place!

1 Work in a group to choose an interesting, fun, or famous place.

2 Write five clues about your place. Then write five questions to ask the other groups about their places.

3 Form a team. Take turns giving clues to the other teams. Let the other teams ask questions.

4 Give clues until a team guesses your place or until all teams have asked all their questions.

Internet Activity

Go to www.sfsocialstudies.com/activities to learn more about Earth.

Working Together

Why is work important?

I'll Work Hard!

by Jackson Ames

 Sung to the tune of "My Bonnie Lies Over the Ocean"

I don't have a pet in my family,
And I want a cat, don't you see?
I'll work hard and save up my income,
Then I'll get a cat just for me!

Work hard, work hard,
I'll work to pay for my cat, my cat!
Work hard, work hard,
I'll work to pay for my cat!

Vocabulary Preview

income

goods

services

tax

TAXES PAY FOR OUR ROADS

FACTORY

FRESH CRAB

HOT CHOWDER

Collect Pay Here

factory

trade

transportation

barter

101

What Will Matt Do?

 Predict

I'm Matt. I want to get my very own cat. If I get a cat, I will feed it and play with it every day.

How can I get a cat? Here are some things I might do.

I can save money to buy a cat at the pet store.

My grandma wants to give me a present. Maybe I can ask her for a cat.

I can ask my parents to take me to an animal shelter to find a cat.

Cats at the animal shelter need good homes. Workers at the animal shelter help people choose the cat that is best for them.

Now it's time for you to predict! **Predict** means to tell what you think will happen next. Think about the things I might do to get a cat. What do you think I will do next?

I decided to ask my mom and dad to take me to the animal shelter. I hope I find a friendly cat! Did I do what you thought I would do?

Try it!

What would happen if the animal shelter did not have any cats? What if Matt's grandmother had already bought him another present? **Predict** what Matt might do next.

Choosing Goods and Services

In the United States, people can make choices about earning, spending, and saving money. People can choose where to work and where to live. Many people choose to live near their jobs.

My mom and dad have jobs. They work hard to earn money. The money that people earn is called **income.** People use their income to pay for different kinds of goods. **Goods** are things people make or grow. Look at the goods in the picture.

Every Saturday, my dad and I go to the grocery store. We buy the food we need.

My dad also uses some of his income to buy services that workers provide. **Services** are jobs that people do to help others. Today we will stop at the barber shop. What does the barber do to help my dad?

Each month, my parents make a budget, a plan for spending and saving their money. First they put aside money to pay for our needs. Needs are things we must have to live.

My family spends some income on wants. Wants are goods and services that people would like to have. We do not need these goods and services to live.

Matt will need a new winter coat.

Let's plan to buy it next month.

My family makes choices about what we can buy. After planning for the things we need, my parents figure out how much money is left.

Then we talk about things we want. We don't have enough money to buy all the things we want. We decide what we want the most. We are going to get a cat!

My family sets aside money to take care of a cat. Then we pick out a cat at the animal shelter. I name her Tabby.

What did you learn?

1. How can jobs help people purchase **goods** and **services?**

2. Explain choices people can make about earning, spending, and saving money.

3. Suppose a person wants to earn **income.** This person likes working outdoors and enjoys taking care of animals. **Predict** where this person might live and work.

Make a Decision

Matt's class painted flower pots and sold them at the craft fair. They made money to buy something for the class. These are the steps they followed when deciding what to buy.

What should we buy?

Step 1 Tell what decision you need to make.

List Your Choices

_ computer
games
_ gerbil
_ books
_ ant farm

108   **Step 2** Gather information.   **Step 3** List your choices.

"Everyone would like new books."

List Your
Choices
computer
games
gerbil
✓books
ant farm

Step 4 Tell what might happen with each choice.

"We made a decision."

Step 5 Make a decision.

Matt's class decided to buy books for the class library. They made a list of the books they want. Now they will buy the books with the money they earned.

What did you learn ?

1. What did Matt's class need to decide?

2. Look at the list of choices. What did Matt's class have to give up when they made their decision to buy books?

3. **On Your Own**
   If you were in Matt's class, what choice would you make? Tell or write about why you think this is the best choice.

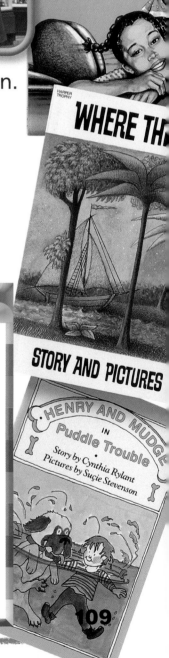

Phoenix Kids Pride Program

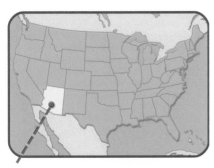

The Phoenix Kids Pride program is found in Phoenix, Arizona.

Meet some children from Phoenix, Arizona. They won a Phoenix Kids Pride Award for helping others in their community and school.

Celso and some of his classmates wanted their school to be a safe place. They talked about how important it is for people to respect each other.

BUILDING
CITIZENSHIP
Caring
Respect
Responsibility
Fairness
Honesty
Courage

With the help of their teachers, Celso and his friends started a special program at their school. Some students went to classes to learn how to help people get along.

Now when students have arguments in the school or on the playground, they spend time with the students who have been trained to help people get along. These students teach other students how to show more respect. They teach them how to settle arguments peacefully.

Good citizens practice respect for others.

Since Celso and his friends started their program, there have been fewer fights and arguments in the school. Students are learning to show respect for each other even when they disagree.

 Respect in Action ⭐

How do these students show that they respect other people? How can you show that you respect the rights of others?

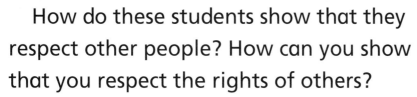

111

Services in Our Community

Our community depends on many people to provide us with important services. Some people teach us, some people care for us, and some people keep us safe.

We are learning about the work people do in our community.

Money that is collected by a government is a **tax.** Taxes help pay for building and repairing schools and other community buildings. Tax money is used to buy fire trucks and police cars too.

Taxes also help pay many of the people who work in our community. We are making a class bulletin board about some of these workers. You can see our bulletin board on the next page.

STOP

ROAD CLOSED

Our mayor and other community leaders help make our community a good place to live.

MAYOR

Firefighters help keep us safe at home and in our community.

Some nurses work in clinics that are paid for by taxes. Many nurses have chosen this work because they want to care for others.

Police officers remind people of important laws that help us live together.

Teachers help us learn. Most teachers work in schools.

What did you learn ?

1. Who do we depend on in our community? What services do they provide?

2. **Predict** what might happen to services and workers in our community if people did not pay their **taxes.**

3. **Think and Share** Write about a job you would like to do. Then draw a picture of a service you would provide or goods you would make for others.

Meet Florence Nightingale

1820–1910
Hospital Reformer and Nurse

Florence Nightingale was a famous nurse. She spent her life serving and caring for others.

Long ago, Florence Nightingale was a leader of nurses. She was in charge of caring for army soldiers during a war. When she arrived at the army hospital, she found it too crowded. The soldiers' clothing was dirty. There were not enough beds.

Florence Nightingale was born in Florence, Italy.

Florence Nightingale was determined to give the soldiers the best care possible. She bought supplies. She worked day and night at the army hospital to care for the soldiers.

After the war, Florence Nightingale started the world's first school of nursing. She wanted nurses to be educated and trained properly.

Florence Nightingale wrote the first textbook for nurses. Florence Nightingale is remembered as the person who trained and encouraged people to be nurses.

Florence Nightingale at work in a hospital

Think and Share

How did Florence Nightingale set an example of good citizenship?

For more information, go online to *Meet the People* at **www.sfsocialstudies.com**.

Fire Engine

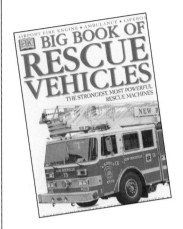

Everyone knows the sound of a fire engine's siren. It warns drivers to move out of the way. There may be a fire, or somebody may be stuck in a tree. Why else might a fire engine be in a hurry?

Two crew members can sit in here.

floodlight

oxygen bottle

fold-down step

118

exhaust pipe

water intake valve

water discharge valve

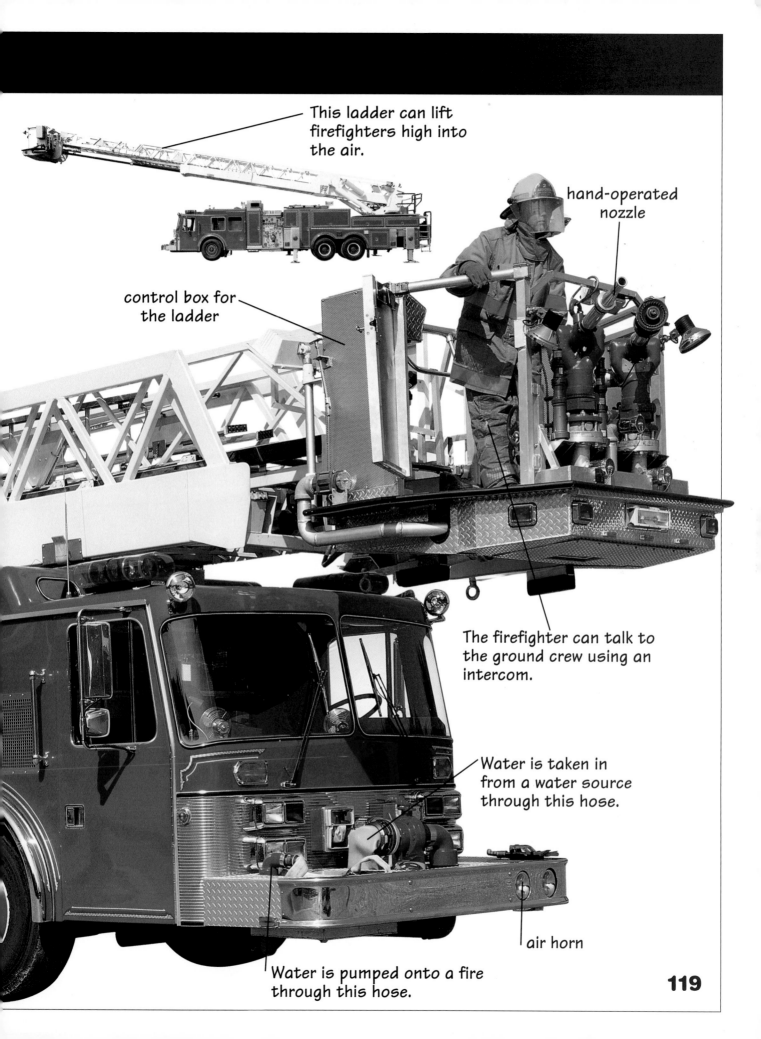

This ladder can lift firefighters high into the air.

hand-operated nozzle

control box for the ladder

The firefighter can talk to the ground crew using an intercom.

Water is taken in from a water source through this hose.

air horn

Water is pumped onto a fire through this hose.

119

3

Goods from the Factory to You

Today, my class is going on a field trip to visit a T-shirt factory. A **factory** is a building where people produce goods. We will learn how people make T-shirts for consumers who will buy them. I get to ask Ken, our tour guide at the factory, questions that my class wrote down.

Matt

What are T-shirts made of?

Ken

Good question! Many T-shirts are made of cotton. Cotton grows on plants. Farmers grow these plants in soil and then harvest the cotton. Long ago, cotton had to be picked by hand. Today, machines do most of the work.

Matt

What happens after the cotton is picked?

Ken

The cotton is taken from the farm to a cotton gin. A cotton gin is a big machine that separates the cotton from its seeds. Then the seedless cotton is packed into bales. Some of these bales are sent to our factory.

Ken Other machines are used to card and spin the cotton fibers into yarn. Then the yarn is knitted or woven into cloth.

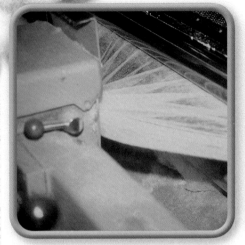

card

spin

knit

Ken The cloth is now dyed and pressed so that it does not have wrinkles. Next workers cut out the pieces to make the T-shirt. Then the pieces of the T-shirt are sewn together.

dye

cut

sew

Matt

When can we buy the T-shirts?

Ken

Not yet! First, the T-shirts are placed into boxes. Next, they are loaded onto trucks. Then, the trucks deliver them to stores all around the country. Last, the T-shirts are unpacked in the stores. Now, consumers can buy a T-shirt.

At the end of the tour, we visited the T-shirt shop. I could buy a T-shirt because I had saved the money I earned from walking my neighbor's dog.

What did you learn?

1. What is a **factory?**

2. Tell how soil, people, and machines are needed to make a T-shirt.

3. **Think and Share** Matt chose to spend the money he earned on a T-shirt. Tell about other choices Matt could have made.

Use a Compass Rose

Find the compass rose on the map.
A **compass rose** shows directions on a map.
The letters N, S, E, and W stand for north,
south, east, and west.

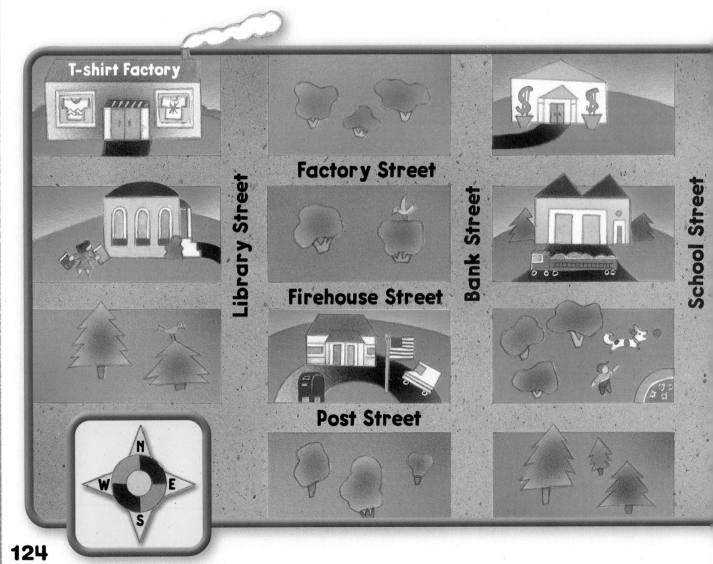

T-shirt Factory

Library Street

Factory Street

Bank Street

School Street

Firehouse Street

Post Street

N
W   E
S

124

One truck from the T-shirt factory went to the Village Store in Matt's community. The truck followed a route. A **route** is a way to go from one place to another. On the map, trace the truck's route.

- Point to the T-shirt Factory.

- Go east on Factory Street.

- Go south on Library Street.

- Go east on Post Street.

- Stop at the Village Store.

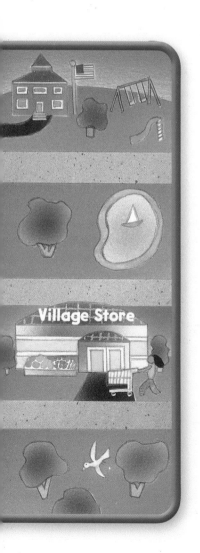

Try it!

1. Is Factory Street north or south of Post Street? Use the **compass rose** to find the answer.

2. Is Library Street east or west of Bank Street?

3. **On Your Own** Write down another **route** you could take from the T-shirt Factory to the Village Store. Ask a classmate to trace your route.

A Trip to the Bank

My family is very proud of me because I saved enough money to buy my T-shirt. I earned income by walking the neighbor's dog. I also helped wash my parents' car. Wow! I worked hard.

I had money left over after buying my T-shirt. I chose to save some of my money. My family took me to the bank to open a savings account.

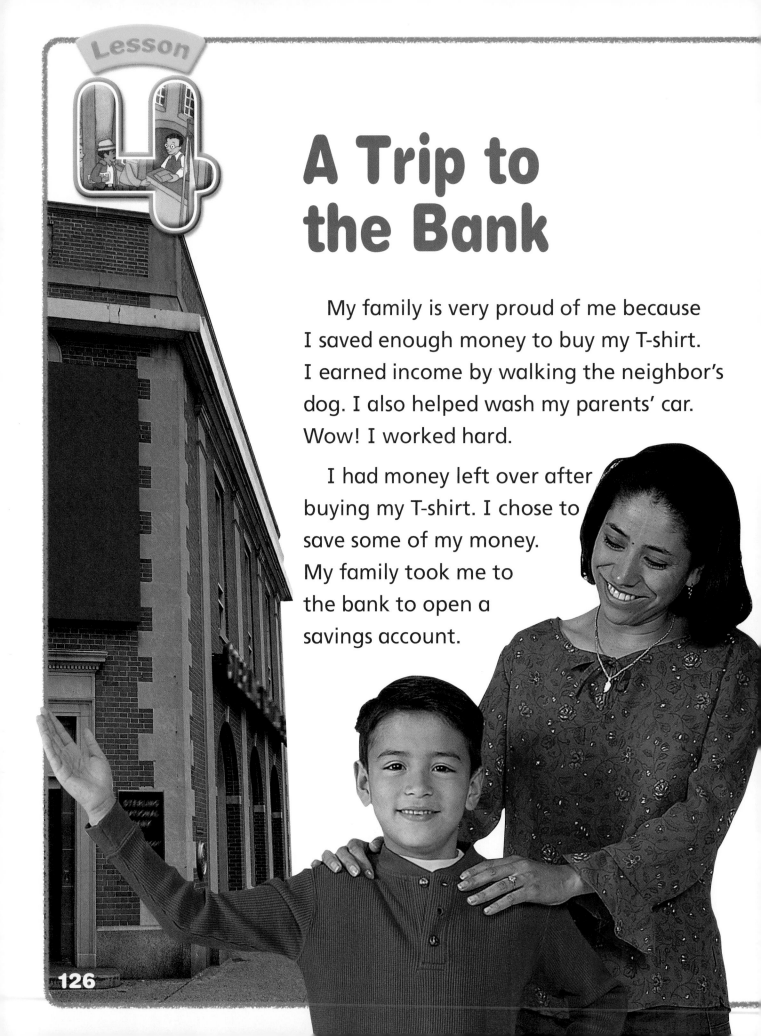

At the bank, we answered questions and signed our names on some papers. When I have income, I will deposit it, or put it into my savings account. Mom or Dad can help me do this at the bank.

My parents also have a checking account. They use the money in their checking account to pay for goods and services.

My mom writes a check at the grocery store. The grocery store sends the check to the bank. The bank takes the money out of my mom's checking account.

Sometimes my parents use a credit card to pay for goods and services. They bought our refrigerator using a credit card. Then they pay their credit card bill at the end of the month.

I work to help my family. Every day I make my bed and set the table. I also work to earn income. Then I can save some of my money and put it into my savings account.

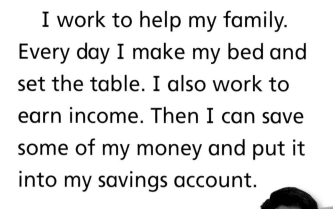

What did you learn?

1. Where can you keep money you want to save?

2. What are different ways people can pay for **goods** and **services?**

3. **Think and Share** Matt wants a new pair of skates. He does not have enough money in his savings account to pay for them. A new neighbor with two dogs moves into Matt's neighborhood. **Predict** what you think Matt will do.

Read a Pie Chart

A **pie chart** is a kind of chart that is drawn in the shape of a circle. The circle is divided into pieces like slices of a pie. The size of a piece shows the amount it stands for.

Savings

T-shirt

Books and Games

Look at the pie chart. You can see how much money Matt decided to save. You can see how he spent his money. Tell what Matt did with the money he earned.

Try it!

1. On what items did Matt spend the same amount of money?

2. Did Matt save more money or spend more on books and games?

3. **On Your Own** Make a **pie chart** that shows another way Matt could spend and save his money.

Meet Linda Alvarado

1951–
Community Leader and Company President

Business owners make careful choices about how to spend and save their money. Linda Alvarado is a successful business owner.

Linda loved school as a little girl. Her family believed that getting an education was very important. She also played sports with her five brothers. She learned the value of teamwork. Education and teamwork have always been important to Linda Alvarado.

When Linda Alvarado was older, she was interested in construction. She liked to visit places where buildings were being built. She took many classes in school that taught her about this business. Finally, she started her own construction company.

Today, Linda Alvarado's company is one of the fastest growing businesses of its kind. She is also one of the owners of a major league baseball team.

Linda Alvarado continues to work hard with her company, baseball team, and community.

Linda Alvarado was born in Albuquerque, New Mexico.

Linda Alvarado

ALVARADO Construction Inc.

Think and Share

What makes Linda Alvarado a successful member of her community?

For more information, go online to *Meet the People* at **www.sfsocialstudies.com.**

Lesson 5

Countries Trade and Move Goods

Rubber is used to make tires for cars, buses, and airplanes.

In my class, we are learning about why countries around the world trade goods. **Trade** means to buy, sell, or exchange goods. Countries need to trade with each other to get goods they do not have.

The United States sells some of the goods we produce, such as wheat and corn, to other countries. We also trade with other countries to get some of the goods we need and want. For example, some companies in the United States buy rubber.

A woman collects a liquid called latex from a rubber tree. The latex is used to make rubber.

Transportation is a way of moving goods or people from place to place. Trains and trucks are two kinds of transportation people can use to send goods over the land. Ships and airplanes are other kinds of transportation people use when they trade goods.

Hot chocolate is one of my favorite treats!

In school, we learned that chocolate is made from cocoa beans. Cocoa beans come from cacao trees. Cacao trees grow best in hot and rainy places. Hawaii is the only state in the United States where cocoa beans grow. There are not enough cocoa beans grown in Hawaii for all our uses. We trade with other countries to get enough cocoa beans.

Cacao tree with pods

The cocoa beans are shipped to factories. Here people and machines make the cocoa beans into chocolate products.

My class made a pie chart of our favorite chocolate products. What product do we like best?

Chocolate Ice Cream

Chocolate Milk

Chocolate Candy

Chocolate Cake

What did you learn ?

1. Tell why countries need to trade with each other.

2. What are some ways that goods could be moved from Europe to the United States?

3. **Think and Share** Look at the label inside a shirt. The label may say where it was made. Tell what kind of **transportation** might have been used to move the shirt to a store near you.

Bartering Goods and Services

Long ago, many people did not use coins and paper bills to buy and sell things. They bartered goods to get what they needed. **Barter** means to trade goods or services for other goods or services without using money.

Today, people still barter. My family sometimes barters services with our neighbors. My dad painted our neighbor's fence. Then our neighbor fixed our car. What other services might people barter?

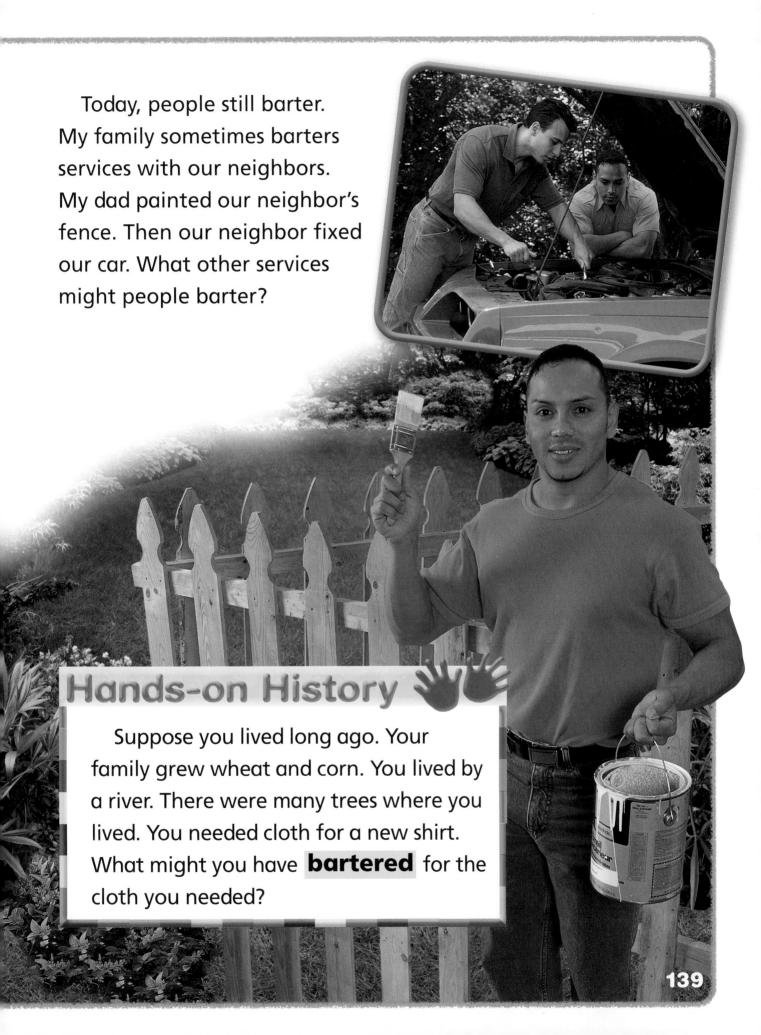

Hands-on History

Suppose you lived long ago. Your family grew wheat and corn. You lived by a river. There were many trees where you lived. You needed cloth for a new shirt. What might you have **bartered** for the cloth you needed?

Can you guess these workers?

I wear heavy boots.
I rhyme with *writer*.
I help you stay safe.
I am a _____ .

I watch from my chair.
My job can be hard.
Look for me at the pool.
I am a _____ .

I help the sick.

Please feel better, not worse.

Look for me at a hospital.

I am a _____ .

I see you most days.

I rhyme with creature.

I help you learn.

I am your _____ !

Review

Vocabulary Review

tax
factory
transportation
income
trade
goods

Match each word to a sentence.

1. This is where goods are made.

2. This is what we earn when we work.

3. This is buying, selling, or exchanging goods.

4. This money pays for some of our schools.

5. This is a way of moving things from place to place.

6. These are things people make or grow.

★ ★ ★ ★ ★ ★ ★ ★

 Which word completes each sentence?

1. To trade goods or services for other goods or services without using money is _____.

    a. transportation   **b.** barter

    c. income   **d.** tax

2. Jobs that people do to help others are _____.

    a. services   **b.** trade

    c. income   **d.** goods

Test Talk

Rule out answers you know are wrong.

Skills Review

Predict

A farmer plants cotton. There is no rain. The cotton plants do not grow. The factory cannot get the cotton it needs to make T-shirts. **Predict** what might happen.

Make a Decision

Think of a decision that you or your classmates might make. Then follow these steps.

1. Tell what decision you need to make.

2. Gather information.

3. List your choices.

4. Tell what might happen with each choice.

5. Make a decision.

Skills Review
Use a Compass Rose

This is a map of buildings and streets in Matt's community. Trace this route on the map.

1. Point to Matt's house.

2. Go east on Willow Way.

3. Go north on Robin Road.

4. Go east on School Street.

5. Tell what building you see.

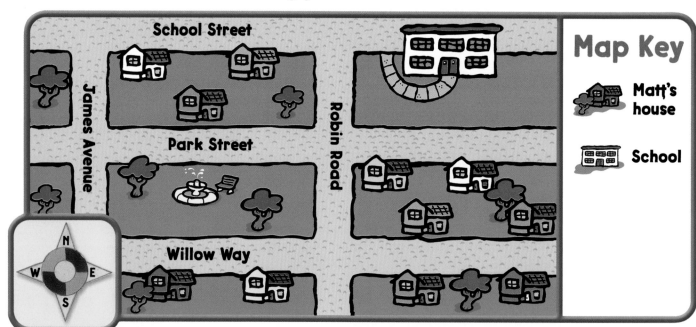

Skills On Your Own

Draw a map of your neighborhood. Put a title and a compass rose on your map. Use the words north, south, east, and west to tell about your map.

What did you learn?

1. What are ways people earn and use their income?

2. How do taxes help a community?

3. Tell how you might barter for goods or services.

4. **Write and Share** Make a list of what a family might choose to buy if they could buy only things that they needed to live.

Read About Work

Look for books like these in the library.

Business Basics

You are going to start a business. A business is a place that sells goods or services. You will advertise its goods or services.

1 **Choose** goods or a service.

2 **Make** a business card for your goods or service.

Top Dog Services

Sam Thomas

3 **Give** your goods or service a name. Write your name and the name of your business on the card.

4 **Share** your business cards with your classmates. See how different each one is.

Internet Activity

Go to www.sfsocialstudies.com/activities to learn more about work.

Our Country Today

Why do we
need government?

Our Country Today

by Alana Sánchez

 Sung to the tune of "Rockabye, Baby"

When people vote
They each make a choice.
We are all citizens.
We have a voice.

We elect people
To serve and to lead.
With honesty and fairness
In action and deed.

149

Vocabulary Preview

government

mayor

citizen

governor

Celebrate America

Capitol

Governor of Ohio Speaking at Noon

Justice For All

Liberty Bell

Learn about Washington, DC

Citizens For Mayor Jones

Justice For All

Washington Monument

Lincoln Memorial

White House

Supreme Court

Jefferson Memorial

George Washington

Susan B. Anthony

Benjamin Banneker

Martin Luther King, Jr.

Congress

President

freedom

motto

monument

151

A Letter to the Editor

Target Skill

Main Idea and Details

Hi! I'm Sam. I wrote a letter about a traffic problem. I sent the letter to my city's newspaper. What is my letter all about?

February 21, 2003

Dear Editor,

I am writing this letter about a traffic problem. We need a stop sign in my neighborhood. I live at the bottom of a hill. I see many people driving down the hill too fast. Children play in my neighborhood. Drivers need to slow down so nobody gets hurt. A stop sign will slow down the cars. Please print this letter so people will know what we need.

Sincerely,
Sam
Second-Grade Student

152

The **topic** tells what the letter is about. The **main idea** is the most important idea about this topic. **Details** tell more about the main idea.

February 21, 2003

Dear Editor,
   I am writing this letter about a traffic problem. We need a stop sign in my neighborhood. I live at the bottom of a hill. I see many people driving down the hill too fast. Children play in my neighborhood. Drivers need to slow down so nobody gets hurt. A stop sign will slow down the cars. Please print this letter so people will know what we need.

Sincerely,
Sam
Second-Grade Student

topic

main idea

detail

detail

detail

Try it!

 Write about something that your neighborhood needs. What is the **topic?** What is the **main idea** about this topic? What are some **details** that tell more about the **main idea?**

Local Government

I want to solve the traffic problem in my neighborhood. My mom and I called our local government for help. A **government** is a group of people who work together to run a city, state, or country. A government provides services, makes laws, helps us stay safe, and settles disagreements.

How can we get a stop sign in our neighborhood?

A **mayor** is the leader of a town or city. The mayor works with a group of people called the city council. The mayor and city council make laws and provide services to their citizens. A **citizen** is a member of a community, state, and country.

The citizens in my community vote to elect our mayor and city council. These leaders, like all citizens, are responsible for doing their jobs and obeying laws. The mayor and city council will help decide if a stop sign is needed in my neighborhood.

Come to the city council meeting in three weeks.

Mayor

My mom set up a neighborhood meeting. We will work together to make our neighborhood a safer place to live.

The local police will help by checking the speed of the cars on our street. If the police catch someone speeding, the person gets a ticket. The person may go to the county courthouse. Here, a judge, or leader of the court, will decide if a law has been broken.

Some government offices are in the county courthouse.

We went to the city council meeting. A police officer gave a report about the speed of the cars on our street. The mayor and city council talked about the problem. Then they voted to put a stop sign in my neighborhood. My neighborhood is now a safer place to live!

What did you learn

1. How did the local **government** help Sam?

2. Tell what a **mayor** and city council do for their town or city.

3. **Think and Share** Write about how the problem in Sam's neighborhood was solved. Include the **topic** and the **main idea.** Include **details** that tell more about the **main idea.**

Anna Beavers lives in Loudoun County, Virginia.

Anna Beavers

Almost 50 years ago, a teacher named Anna Beavers decided to solve a problem in her community. Some children needed better clothes to wear to school.

Mrs. Beavers saw children come to school in clothes that were dirty or torn. Children judged unfairly and made fun of these children because of the clothes they wore.

BUILDING CITIZENSHIP
Caring
Respect
Responsibility
Fairness
Honesty
Courage

Mrs. Beavers decided to wash and mend these clothes. If the clothes were too ragged to mend, Mrs. Beavers bought new clothes. She wanted all of the children to have nice clothes. Today, Mrs. Beavers is still helping children look good and feel good about themselves.

Although Mrs. Beavers is retired, she continues helping children in her Virginia community. She mends clothes. She teaches children who are sick or behind in school. Anna Beavers respects people, including children, and is very caring. She does good deeds for others and believes in fairness for all.

 Fairness in Action

What can you do to treat others fairly?

159

State Government

I live in the state of California. Every state has its own government. The **governor** is the leader of a state's government. The governor works with other state leaders. The citizens of each state vote to elect their leaders.

Every state also has its own capital. The capital of California is Sacramento. This is the city where many leaders of our state live and work. The capitol building is where leaders meet to make the laws for our state. Find the capital of California on the map. It is marked with a star.

California

Map Key

⭐ State Capital

◉ City

⬤ Ocean

--- Border

Sacramento ⭐

San Francisco ◌

Los Angeles ◌

San Diego ◌

PACIFIC OCEAN

Government collects tax money to pay for services in our communities. Then the governor and other leaders make a budget to decide how to use the tax money. They want to spend the money they have for community services needed by citizens. We drew pictures of some things taxes help pay for in our community.

School

Library

Park

Schools, libraries, and parks make our communities better places to live.

My class made posters about our local and state governments. Who makes laws for my state?

I want to be a great leader!

My City

- Mayor and City Council
  They make laws.
- Local Police
  They carry out laws.
- Local Court
  They decide if laws are broken.

My State

- Governor and State Leaders
  They make laws.
- State Police
  They carry out laws.
- State Court
  They decide if laws are broken.

Someday, I'd like to be a government leader. Maybe I'll be mayor. I can help run my city. Maybe I'll be governor. Then I can help run my state!

What did you learn?

1. How are the jobs of a **mayor** and **governor** alike? How are they different?

2. Name some service the **government** provides for your community.

3. **Think and Share** Tell why it is important for governments to make laws and see that these laws are followed.

Read a Table

Look at the table. A **table** is a kind of list.
A table gives information that people can use.

Learn About States

State	State Capital	State Bird	State Flower
Florida	Tallahassee	Mockingbird	Orange Blossom
Alabama	Montgomery	Yellowhammer	Camellia
Ohio	Columbus	Cardinal	Scarlet Carnation

This table lists important facts about some of our states. Each state has a capital city. Each capital city has a capitol building where the state lawmakers meet.

States also have symbols. These symbols help us understand what makes each state special. The state bird and the state flower are two symbols of our states.

Try it!

1. What is the capital of Alabama?

2. What is Florida's state flower?

3. **On Your Own** Learn about the capital, state bird, and state flower of your state. Make a **table** showing this information. Include a drawing of your state's capitol building.

Federal Government

The Constitution was written more than 200 years ago.

The government in our country works for all of the people in the country. The government follows a plan that was written long ago. This plan for government is called the United States Constitution.

The Constitution

We the People

Article I.

166

The center of our government is in Washington, D.C., our country's capital. The United States government has three parts. Our country needs all of the parts to make government work fairly.

One part of government is Congress. The **Congress** writes and votes on laws for all of our states. Citizens from each state elect leaders to be in Congress. These leaders are called lawmakers because they make laws.

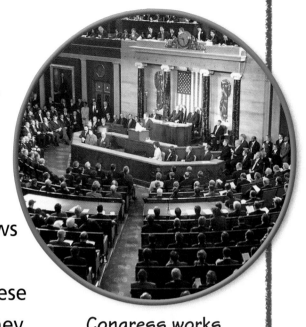

Congress works in the United States Capitol.

United States Capitol

The President heads another part of government. The **President** is the leader of our country. Citizens from every state vote for our President. The President signs laws. The President works with leaders from other countries. Who is our President?

The President lives and works in the White House.

Another part of government is the Supreme Court. There are nine judges called Supreme Court justices. The President chooses the justices, but one part of Congress must approve the President's choices.

The Supreme Court tells us if laws are fair. They also decide if laws have been broken. The justices use the United States Constitution as their guide.

Supreme Court Building

Sandra Day O'Connor became the first woman Supreme Court Justice in 1981.

What did you learn?

1. How are the jobs of a **mayor,** a **governor,** and the **President** alike? How are they different?

2. How does a person become a Supreme Court justice?

3. **Think and Share** Think about the three parts of **government.** Write to tell which one you would choose to work in and why.

Meet Thurgood Marshall

1908–1993
Supreme Court Justice

Thurgood Marshall was the first African American justice on the Supreme Court. He fought for the rights of all Americans.

As a young boy, Thurgood's father would take him to the courthouse to watch trials. Thurgood and his brother attended college in Pennsylvania. Then Thurgood applied to law school but was turned down because he was an African American. This event led him to spend the rest of his life working for equal rights. He was accepted at another law school, where he graduated at the top of his class.

Thurgood Marshall was born in Baltimore, Maryland.

Supreme Court justices, 1967

As a lawyer, Thurgood Marshall brought many cases before the Supreme Court. In one case, black children could not go to school with white children. This case was about segregation. Segregation means that people are kept apart because of the color of their skin. Thurgood Marshall won this case.

Thurgood Marshall was chosen to become a Supreme Court justice. He continued to work for fair and equal treatment for all people.

Thurgood Marshall

Think and Share

How did Thurgood Marshall help all Americans to be treated equally and fairly?

For more information, go online to *Meet the People* at **www.sfsocialstudies.com**.

Re-ELECT OUR MAYOR

Voting for Leaders

KEEP AMERICA STRONG

Our class is learning about how we choose leaders. Next week, we will vote for a class leader. What makes a good leader? What do you know about voting?

Every American citizen who is at least 18 years old has the right to vote. First a citizen must sign up to vote. Then citizens learn about the people who are running for office.

VOTE NOW

Sign Up Here

Citizens make decisions about who they want as their leaders. They ask themselves many questions. Who will do the best job? Can I trust the person? Will this person work hard to make our country a better place to live and work? You may have talked with your family about how to choose a leader.

My parents read the newspaper to get information.

They watch television programs about the people running for office.

They talk to friends and neighbors about important issues.

They use the computer to learn more about these issues.

When it's time for the election, citizens vote. First, they get a ballot. A ballot lists the names of people running for different offices. Next, each citizen marks his or her choices on the ballot. Last, each vote gets counted.

My mom is getting a ballot.

My mom knows voting is important.

My mom helps elect government leaders. Elected leaders have an important job to do. I can help elect my class leader. I can also vote to make classroom decisions.

KEEP AMERICA STRONG

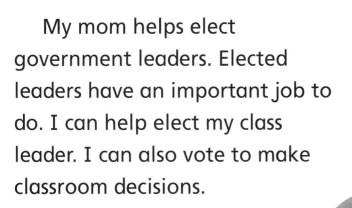

What did you learn?

1. How can a **citizen** of our country who is at least 18 years old help elect a leader?

2. Name three ways you could learn more about a candidate.

3. **Think and Share** Think of reasons why a person is a good leader. Write a story about a leader.

Leaders and Lawmakers

Our country has many laws. The men and women who make our laws are called lawmakers. We have voted for our lawmakers for most of our history.

The United States Congress

The first meeting of lawmakers in English-speaking North America was in 1619. They met in Jamestown, Virginia.

Many Americans in the 1770s thought British laws were not fair. They voted for leaders in 1776. These leaders wrote the Declaration of Independence. It said Americans were free. It created the United States.

In 1789, Americans chose George Washington as their first President and voted for the country's first group of lawmakers.

The people who make laws for our country make up the Congress. Each state sends lawmakers to Congress. Find out about a lawmaker from your state. List some facts about how he or she got to Congress.

Meet
Susan B. Anthony

1820–1906
Equal Rights Leader

Susan B. Anthony helped women get the right to vote. She was the first woman to be pictured on United States money.

WOMEN'S RIGHTS

WOMEN'S RIGHTS

Susan B. Anthony lived during a time when men and women were not treated equally. Women were not allowed to vote. Many women did not go to school.

Susan's family was interested in her education. Susan learned to read and write at the age of three. When she was older, her family found a college that allowed women to attend. Susan became a teacher.

Susan B. Anthony believed that women should have the same rights as men. She believed that women should have the right to vote. She voted in the 1872 presidential election. She was arrested and fined. She refused to pay the fine.

Susan B. Anthony traveled around the country, talking about women's rights. She spoke at meetings and wrote books. Her hard work led to amending, or changing, the United States Constitution. In 1920, women were allowed to vote for the first time.

Susan B. Anthony was born in Adams, Massachusetts.

Susan B. Anthony seated at her desk

Susan B. Anthony dollar coin

Think and Share

How did Susan B. Anthony work to improve the lives of American citizens?

For more information, go online to *Meet the People* at www.sfsocialstudies.com.

The Land of Freedom

Many people in our country have fought for freedom.

Freedom is every citizen's right to make choices. The Bill of Rights is a list of freedoms for all Americans. It is an important part of our Constitution.

Our country's national anthem, or song, is called "The Star-Spangled Banner." The last part says that we live in ". . . the land of the free and the home of the brave."

Bill of Rights

Congress OF THE United States,

begun and held at the City of New York, on Wednesday, the fourth of March, one thousand seven hundred and eighty nine.

The Conventions of a number of the States having, at the time of their adopting the Constitution, expressed a desire, in order to prevent misconstruction or abuse of its powers, that further declaratory and restrictive clauses should be added: And as extending the ground of public confidence in the Government, will best insure the beneficent ends of its institution:

Resolved, by the SENATE and HOUSE of REPRESENTATIVES of the UNITED STATES of AMERICA in Congress assembled, two thirds of both Houses concurring, That the following Articles be proposed to the Legislatures of the several States, as Amendments to the Constitution of the United States; all, or any of which articles, when ratified by three fourths of the said Legislatures, to be valid to all intents and purposes, as part of the said Constitution, viz.

Articles in addition to, and Amendment of the Constitution of the United States of America, proposed by Congress, and ratified by the Legislatures of the several States, pursuant to the fifth Article of the Original Constitution.

Article the first ...... After the first enumeration required by the first Article of the Constitution, there shall be one Representative for every thirty thousand, until the number shall amount to one hundred, after which, the proportion shall be so regulated by Congress, that there shall be not less than one hundred Representatives, nor less than one Representative for every forty thousand persons, until the number of Representatives shall amount to two hundred, after which, the proportion shall be so regulated by Congress, that there shall not be less than two hundred Representatives, nor more than one Representative for every fifty thousand persons. [Not Ratified]

Article the second .... No law, varying the compensation for the services of the Senators and Representatives, shall take effect, until an election of Representatives shall have intervened. [Not Ratified]

Article the third .... Congress shall make no law respecting an establishment of religion, or prohibiting the free exercise thereof; or abridging the freedom of speech, or of the press; or the right of the people peaceably to assemble, and to petition the Government for a redress of grievances.

Article the fourth ..... A well regulated Militia, being necessary to the security of a free State, the right of the people to keep and bear Arms, shall not be infringed.

Article the fifth .... No Soldier shall, in time of peace, be quartered in any house, without the consent of the owner, nor in time of war, but in a manner to be prescribed by law.

Article the sixth .... The right of the people to be secure in their persons, houses, papers, and effects, against unreasonable searches and seizures, shall not be violated, and no Warrants shall issue but upon probable cause, supported by oath or affirmation, and particularly describing the place to be searched, and the persons or things to be seized.

Article the seventh ... No person shall be held to answer for a capital, or otherwise infamous crime, unless on a presentment or indictment of a grand jury, except in

A **motto** is a word or saying that people try to live by. The motto *Liberty* means "freedom." The motto *E Pluribus Unum* means "out of many, one." Americans are many people who live in one country.

We have symbols that stand for our country too. The rose is our national flower. Here are other symbols I have made.

The Liberty Bell celebrates our freedom.

The bald eagle is our national bird.

Uncle Sam is a symbol for the United States of America.

George Washington was the first President of the United States. He helped the new government work for all of the people. Thomas Jefferson and Abraham Lincoln were other important Presidents.

Our country built monuments to remember these Presidents. A **monument** is a building or statue that honors a person or an event. The Washington Monument and the Lincoln and Jefferson Memorials are located in Washington, D.C.

George Washington

Abraham Lincoln

Thomas Jefferson

Dr. Martin Luther King, Jr., wanted all people to be treated fairly. For a long time African Americans were treated unfairly because of the color of their skin. Dr. King made speeches and led peaceful marches. He is remembered on Martin Luther King, Jr., Day in January each year.

What did you learn?

1. Tell what you think it would be like to live in a country that did not have our **freedoms.**

2. Name two symbols and one **motto** that stand for our country.

3. **Think and Share** Write about the **topic** of a famous American. Begin with your **main idea.** Add **details** that tell more about your **main idea.**

Use a Map Grid

Look at this map of Washington, D.C.
Many of the buildings and monuments you
are learning about can be found on this map.

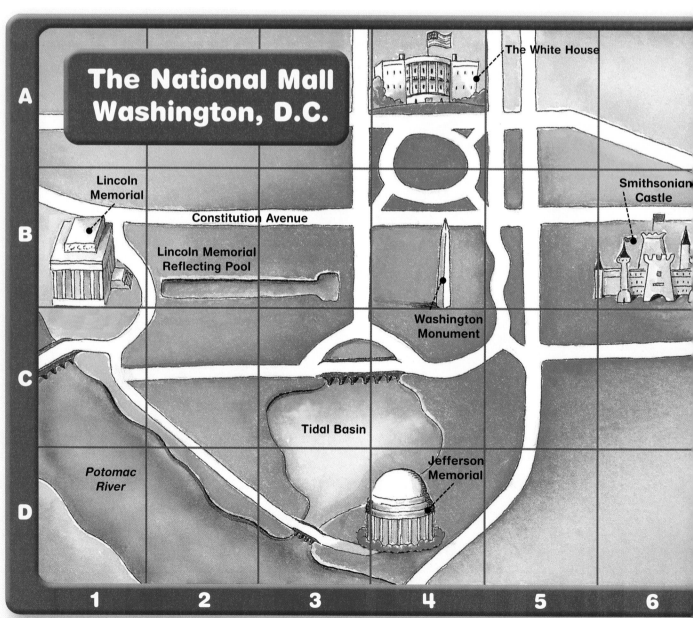

The National Mall
Washington, D.C.

The White House

Lincoln Memorial

Smithsonian Castle

Constitution Avenue

Lincoln Memorial Reflecting Pool

Washington Monument

Tidal Basin

Potomac River

Jefferson Memorial

A B C D

1 2 3 4 5 6

This map has a grid. A **grid** is a pattern of lines that form squares. The squares have numbers and letters. You can use a grid to find places on the map. Point to the Lincoln Memorial. It is in square B-1. Point to the Smithsonian Castle. Name this square's letter and number.

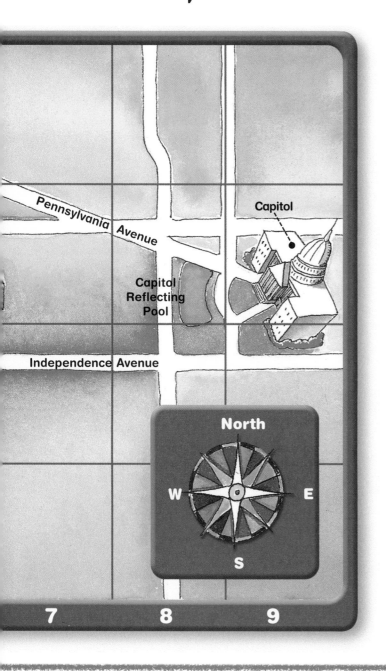

Pennsylvania Avenue

Capitol

Capital Reflecting Pool

Independence Avenue

North

W   E

S

7   8   9

Try it!

1. Find the White House on the map **grid.** Tell the square's letter and number.

2. What is found in square B-4?

3. **On Your Own** Point to the White House. Move south three squares. What is the name of the building in this square? What is its letter and number?

Flags Around the World

Sam and his class are learning about flags from other countries. Each flag has different colors and designs that represent its country.

Canada: This country has many maple trees. Find the red maple leaf on the flag.

Brazil: Find the globe in the center. The stars are arranged to look like the night sky over Brazil.

NORTH AMERICA

ATLANTIC OCEAN

AFRICA

PACIFIC OCEAN

SOUTH AMERICA

N

W   E

S

The American flag is red, white, and blue. The stars stand for each of our 50 states. The stripes stand for the first 13 states in the United States.

For more information, go online to the *Atlas* at **www.sfsocialstudies.com.**

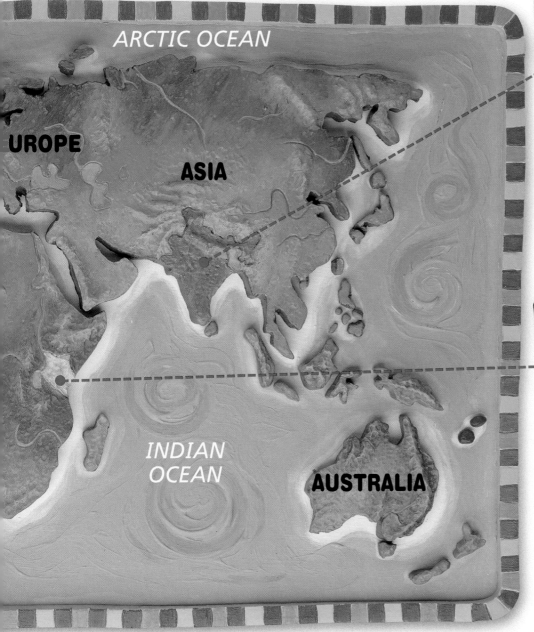

ARCTIC OCEAN

EUROPE

ASIA

INDIAN OCEAN

AUSTRALIA

India: There are three stripes of orange-yellow, white, and green. The symbol in the center is a *Dharma chakra*, or wheel.

Kenya: This flag has three wide stripes. Find the warrior's shield and spears at the center of the flag.

187

End with a Song

You're a Grand Old Flag

by George M. Cohan

You're a grand old flag,
You're a high flying flag
And forever in peace may you wave.
You're the emblem of the land I love.
The home of the free and the brave.

Ev'ry heart beats true
'Neath the red, white, and blue,
Where there's never a boast or brag.
Should auld acquaintance be forgot,
Keep your eye on the grand old flag.

Vocabulary Review

motto
freedom
monument
citizen
President

Tell which word completes each sentence.

1. Every citizen's right to make choices is a _____.

2. A word or saying that people try to live by is a _____.

3. The leader of our country is the _____.

4. A statue that honors a person is a _____.

5. A member of a community, state, or country is a _____.

★ ★ ★ ★ ★ ★ ★ ★

 Which word completes each sentence?

1. A group of people who work together to run a city, state, or country is a _____.

   a. government   **b.** Congress

   c. President   **d.** mayor

2. The _____ writes and votes on laws for our country.

   a. mayor   **b.** governor

   c. President   **d.** Congress

Skills Review

Main Idea and Details

Write about a symbol that stands for our country. Put your **main idea** in the first sentence. Put **details** that support your **main idea** in other sentences.

Read a Table

Look at the table to answer these questions.

1. Which flag shows a grizzly bear?

2. Which state is called the Lone Star State?

State	Flag	About the Flag
Texas		This is called the Lone Star Flag.
California		The grizzly bear stands for courage.
South Carolina		The palmetto tree is on this state flag.
Montana		The state seal is in the center of this flag.
Indiana		The flaming torch stands for liberty.

Skills Review

Use a Map Grid

Read the grid map to answer these questions.

1. In which square is the State Capitol?

2. What is in square C-3?

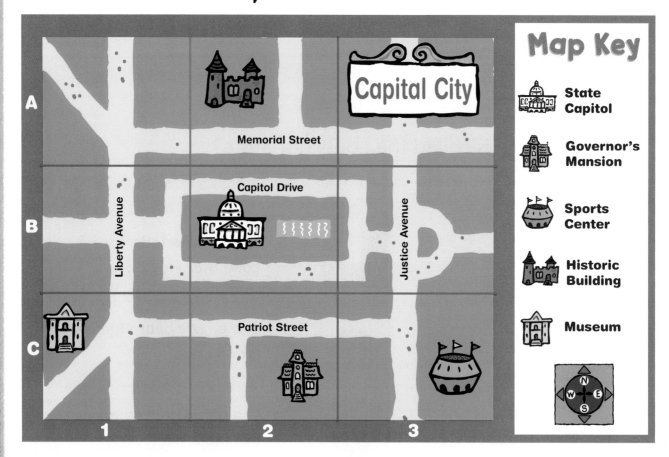

Skills On Your Own

Make a map of your classroom. Put a grid on your map. Use the grid to tell the location of something on your map.

What did you learn?

1. Why do we need government?

2. Explain why libraries, schools, and parks are important to a community.

3. Why do you think it is important for citizens to vote?

4. **Write and Share** Write about the following **topic:** What people in government do. Put your **main idea** in the first sentence. Write other sentences that give **details** about the **main idea.**

Test Talk

Look for details to support your answer.

Read About Your Country

Look for books like these in the library.

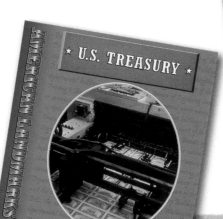

193

UNIT 4 Project

Get Out the Vote

Elections are important. Now is your chance to campaign for your own candidate.

Arthur for President

1 Work as a class and choose an office for your election.

2 Divide into groups. In your group, choose a character from a book to run for the office.

3 Draw a campaign poster for your candidate. Write a campaign commercial for your candidate. Explain to the class why your candidate is the best choice.

4 Vote for the best candidate.

Internet Activity

Go to www.sfsocialstudies.com/activities to learn more about our country today.

Our Country Long Ago

Why is it important to learn about our country's history?

195

Living in America

by Henry Delaney

Sung to the tune of
"Skip to My Lou"

Long ago they sailed the sea,
Traveled far with family,
Built homes in each colony.
They came to America.

Soon they wanted to be free,
Living independently.
Fighting for their liberty,
Living in America.

Vocabulary Preview

shelter

tradition

explorer

colony

People in History

Christopher Columbus

Lewis & Clark and Sacagawea

Oregon Trail

4th of July

Declaration of Independence

13 Colonies

New York
New Jersey
New Hampshire
Maryland
Delaware
Rhode Island

North Carolina
South Carolina
Virginia
Pennsylvania
Georgia
Massachusetts
Connecticut

colonist

independence

pioneer

Mara's Project

Put Things in Order

Target Skill

Hi, my name is Mara. I am working on a project about the Pueblo people. As you read about my project, look for clue words that tell the order in which things happen. **First, next,** and **last** are clue words.

First, I went to the library and looked for books. I checked out books to help with my project.

Next, I read the books and drew pictures to show how the Pueblo people live.

Last, I told my class about what I learned. I showed them my pictures.

Now look at these pictures. Tell what I did.
Use the clue words **first, next,** and **last.**

First   **Next**   **Last**

Try it!

 Tell about how you get ready for school. Use the clue words **first, next,** and **last.** Draw pictures to show the order in which things happen.

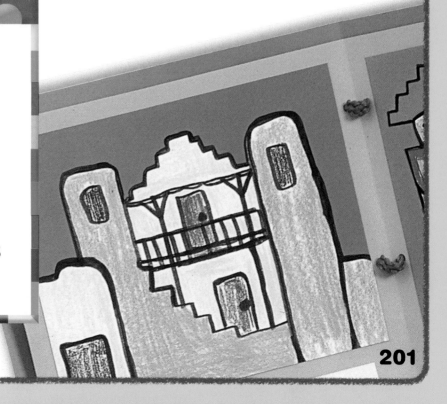

The First Americans

Native American groups lived in many different places.

My class is learning about Native Americans. Look at this map. It shows where three of the many Native American groups lived long ago. Some still live in these parts of the United States today.

Native American Groups

Atlantic Ocean

N
W   E
S

Map Key

Pueblo land
Sioux land
Powhatan land
Present-day United States borders

We made a table that tells about Native American culture, or way of life. Each group used the resources around them to make their food, clothing, and shelter. A **shelter** is a place where people live.

Native American Groups

	Food	Clothing	Shelter	Transportation
Powhatan	deer, fish, nuts, berries, corn	made from hides of animals	longhouse	walked, used canoes
Sioux	buffalo	made of buffalo hides	tepee	walked, rode horses
Pueblo	corn, beans, squash	made of cotton fibers	adobe buildings	walked

The Powhatan

Many Powhatan lived along the Atlantic coast. The winters were mild and the summers were hot. The men fished and hunted. They made canoes out of trees. The women gathered and grew the food. The women also built the homes and cared for their children.

Powhatan children listened to legends and stories and played games. One game was played to see who could count sticks fastest.

Powhatan bowl

The Sioux

Many Sioux lived on the grassy plains. The winters were very cold and the summers were hot. The Sioux hunted buffalo for making food, clothing, and homes.

The Sioux who hunted needed homes that they could take down quickly. They moved often to hunt for buffalo. They made tepees. First, they tied long poles together. Next, the bottoms of the poles were spread out to make a circle. Last, they covered the poles with buffalo hides.

204

Sioux painted buffalo robe

The Pueblo

Many Pueblo people lived in the dry desert of the Southwest. There were few wild plants to gather or animals to hunt for food. Some Pueblo farmed.

The Pueblo lived in villages in stone or adobe homes. Clay bricks that are baked in the sun are called adobe.

The Pueblo made clay pots to store food and water. Clay pots are still made by some Pueblo people.

Pueblo farmers watching their crops

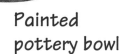

Painted pottery bowl

What did you learn?

1. Look at the map on page 202. Which Native American group is closest to the Atlantic Ocean?

2. Look at the table on page 203. Explain how each group used the resources around them to meet their needs.

3. Tell how the Sioux people made tepees. Use the clue words **first, next,** and **last** to tell the order in which things happen.

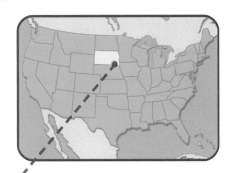

Ella Cara Deloria was born on the Yankton Sioux reservation in South Dakota.

Ella Cara Deloria

Ella was born on a Sioux reservation in South Dakota. The people on her reservation were also called Dakota. She was given the Dakota name Anpetu Waste. In English, this name means Beautiful Day.

Ella spoke Sioux before she learned English. Her parents wanted her to have a good education. She went away to school. Later, she went to college to become a teacher.

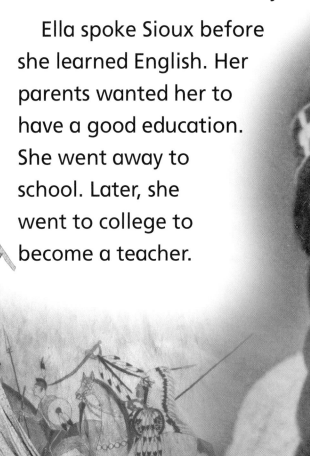

BUILDING
CITIZENSHIP
Caring
Respect
Responsibility
Fairness
★ Honesty
Courage

Ella Cara Deloria studied the culture, or way of life, of the Sioux people. Because she was an honest person and spoke the language, the Sioux trusted her. They spoke with her about their families and their ceremonies. Storytellers shared stories of their ancestors.

Ella Cara Deloria wrote many books about the Sioux language and culture. In *Waterlily,* she tells the story of a young Dakota woman. She also wrote about Sioux traditions. A **tradition** is something that is done a certain way for many years. She wanted to keep the Sioux traditions alive.

Ella Cara Deloria

Ella Cara Deloria is remembered as a person who wrote truthful accounts of the history of her community. She helped others understand the culture of the Sioux people.

★ Honesty in Action ★

Why do you think it was important for Ella Cara Deloria to be honest in what she said and wrote? How can you practice honesty?

Native Americans Meet English Colonists

Colonists from England liked Native American goods. They brought goods from England to trade. Native Americans liked English goods. They traded. Life changed for Native Americans with these new goods.

This drawing shows how Native Americans might have looked when the English first came to Virginia. An Englishman drew it in 1590.

208

Here are some of the goods that the English brought with them:

Firearms, such as this trade gun ▲

▲ Powderhorns to hold gunpowder

◄ Cloth and clothing items, such as this shirt

Beads to go on clothing and on moccasins ▼

Metal goods, such as this cooking kettle and ax

Do some research on your own. Tell how trade was important to the English and the Native Americans. How did trade change how the Native Americans lived?

Colonies

Explorers from Europe sailed across the Atlantic Ocean and landed on the shores of North America. An **explorer** is a person who travels to a new place to learn about it. Christopher Columbus was an explorer. He sailed to the Americas.

Explorers from Spain reached Florida while searching for gold. They built a Spanish colony there called St. Augustine. A **colony** is a place that is settled by people from another country. Soon more people from Spain came to live in North America.

Spanish gold coin

St. Augustine is the oldest European community in the United States.

Later, English colonists settled Jamestown. A **colonist** is a person who lives in a colony. England ruled the Jamestown colonists.

The Jamestown colonists had hard times. Many of them became ill. They did not have enough food. They did not know how to farm the new land. Some colonists spent their time looking for gold instead of food.

A leader named John Smith helped the Jamestown colonists become better workers. The colonists cleared land, built homes, planted crops, and hunted for food. They traded with the Powhatan people for corn.

Other people wanted to live in our country too.

Jamestown Fort

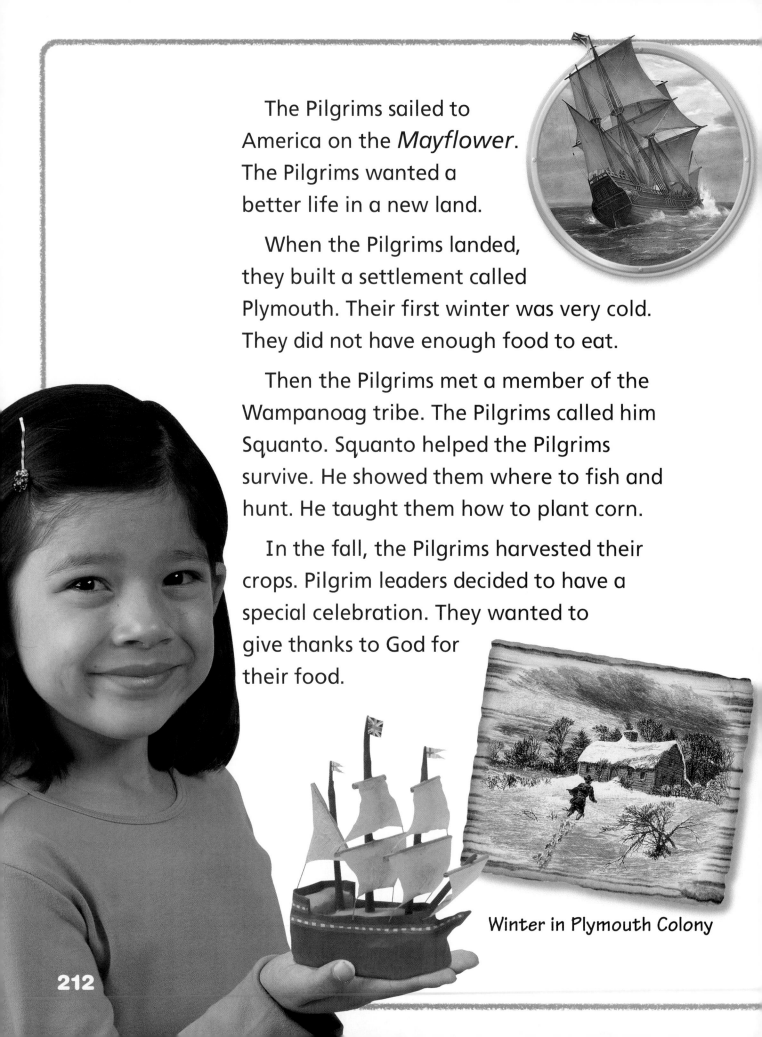

The Pilgrims sailed to America on the *Mayflower*. The Pilgrims wanted a better life in a new land.

When the Pilgrims landed, they built a settlement called Plymouth. Their first winter was very cold. They did not have enough food to eat.

Then the Pilgrims met a member of the Wampanoag tribe. The Pilgrims called him Squanto. Squanto helped the Pilgrims survive. He showed them where to fish and hunt. He taught them how to plant corn.

In the fall, the Pilgrims harvested their crops. Pilgrim leaders decided to have a special celebration. They wanted to give thanks to God for their food.

Winter in Plymouth Colony

The Pilgrims invited the Wampanoag to their celebration. They probably ate foods like cornbread and turkey, danced, and played games. Later, this celebration was called Thanksgiving.

Thanksgiving celebration

Today, Thanksgiving is a national holiday. Thanksgiving is celebrated on the fourth Thursday in November. It is a time when we give thanks for our family and friends. How do you celebrate Thanksgiving?

What did you learn ?

1. How was life hard for the Jamestown **colonists?**

2. Why is Thanksgiving an important holiday?

3. **Think and Share** Write about how Squanto helped the Pilgrims.

213

Use a Map Scale

Look at the map of a Pilgrim house. This map shows distance. **Distance** is the amount of space between two things. You can use a **map scale** to find the distance between two places.

A Pilgrim House

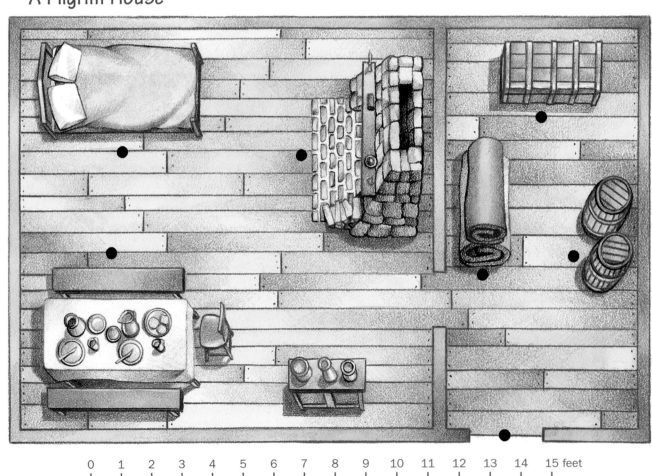

Place a strip of paper from the dot by the bed to the dot by the fireplace. Be sure the edge of the paper touches each dot. Mark where each dot is on the paper. Then place the paper on the map scale. Be sure one of the marks on the paper is at zero. Tell the distance between the bed and the fireplace.

House at Plymouth

What did you learn?

1. Tell how to find the **distance** between the two barrels and the door.

2. How far is the bed from the table?

3. **On Your Own** Make a map of the hall between your classroom and the classroom next to yours. Show a **map scale** with your map.

For more information, go online to the *Atlas* at **www.sfsocialstudies.com**.

Thirteen Colonies, One Country

Here is a map of the 13 colonies.

Many more people from England and other countries came to live in America after the colonists in Jamestown and the Pilgrims in Plymouth. Soon there were 13 colonies.

The colonies were still ruled by England. There were laws that many of the colonists did not like. The colonists had to pay taxes that they thought were unfair.

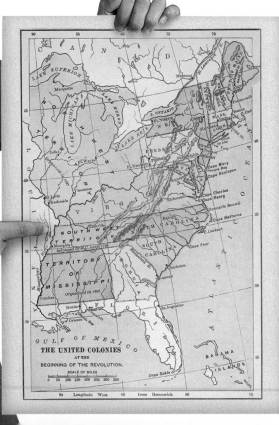

English Colonies, 1775

The colonies began working as one united
colony instead of 13 separate colonies. Patrick
Henry was a colonist from Virginia. He said,
"I am not a Virginian, but an American."

Most of the colonists wanted their
independence from England. **Independence**
means to be free from other people or places.
Thomas Jefferson was chosen to write the
Declaration of Independence. The Declaration
of Independence was approved on July 4, 1776.
The colonies were becoming one country, the
United States of America.

217

George Washington became our country's first President.

England did not want to give the colonies independence. Many colonists were willing to fight England to be free. Some colonists, however, chose to be loyal to England.

The American Revolution began. George Washington was chosen to be the leader of the army. France and Spain agreed to help the United States. The war was long and hard. In the end, the Americans won their independence.

George Washington at Valley Forge

My family and I celebrate Independence Day on July 4 each year. It is the holiday that honors our country's birthday. On Independence Day, we celebrate our country's freedom. It is a tradition in my family to go to a parade, have a picnic, and watch fireworks. How do you celebrate?

What did you learn?

1. Why did many Americans want their **independence** from England?

2. What did George Washington do during the American Revolution?

3. **Think and Share** Write about why it is important for Americans to remember July 4, 1776.

219

Meet
Paul Revere

1735–1818
Patriot and Silversmith

Paul Revere was a hero to the Americans before the Revolutionary War began. He warned people that the British troops were coming.

Paul Revere was a patriot. Patriot was the name given to a colonist who wanted independence from England. In 1775, Paul Revere learned that the English troops in Boston were going to march through the countryside. He and his friends made a secret signal to let Americans know. Two lanterns would be placed in Boston's North Church steeple. One lantern would be lit if the English left Boston by land. Two lanterns would be lit if the English left Boston by sea.

Two lanterns were seen on the night of April 18, 1775. Paul Revere rode from Boston to a town called Lexington. He and another rider reached Lexington in time to warn others so they could escape before the English troops arrived.

Paul Revere is remembered as a patriot and a craftsman. He is also remembered in a poem called "Paul Revere's Ride."

Paul Revere was born in Boston, Massachusetts.

North Church

Paul Revere made beautiful silverware.

Think and Share

How did Paul Revere show that he felt responsible for the safety of the colonists?

For more information, go online to *Meet the People* at **www.sfsocialstudies.com.**

Our Country Grows

Thomas Jefferson, the third President of the United States, wanted to explore the West. The United States bought a huge area of land in the West from the French. President Jefferson sent a group of people to find a way to the Pacific Ocean.

First, the explorers set out from St. Louis, Missouri. Meriwether Lewis and William Clark led the explorers. They traveled up the Missouri River.

Next, Lewis and Clark met a Shoshone woman named Sacagawea. She helped the explorers find food. Sacagawea also helped the explorers talk to other Native Americans they met along the way.

Last, Lewis and Clark led the explorers across the Rocky Mountains. They continued on until they saw the Pacific Ocean.

Lewis and Clark returned to St. Louis. The trip had lasted about two and a half years. Lewis and Clark drew maps and wrote journals about their trip.

William Clark's diary

Lewis and Clark's Route

Columbia River

Fort Mandan

Missouri River

Mississippi River

Lewis

Clark

St. Louis

ROCKY MOUNTAINS

PACIFIC OCEAN

What could you fit into a covered wagon?

People called pioneers led the way west. A **pioneer** is a person who goes first and prepares the way for others. The pioneers went west because they wanted to own land and build homes. Many pioneers settled land west of the Mississippi River.

The pioneers traveled west in many ways. Some walked or rode horses. Many families traveled in covered wagons. They put everything that would fit into the wagon. If something did not fit, they would leave it behind.

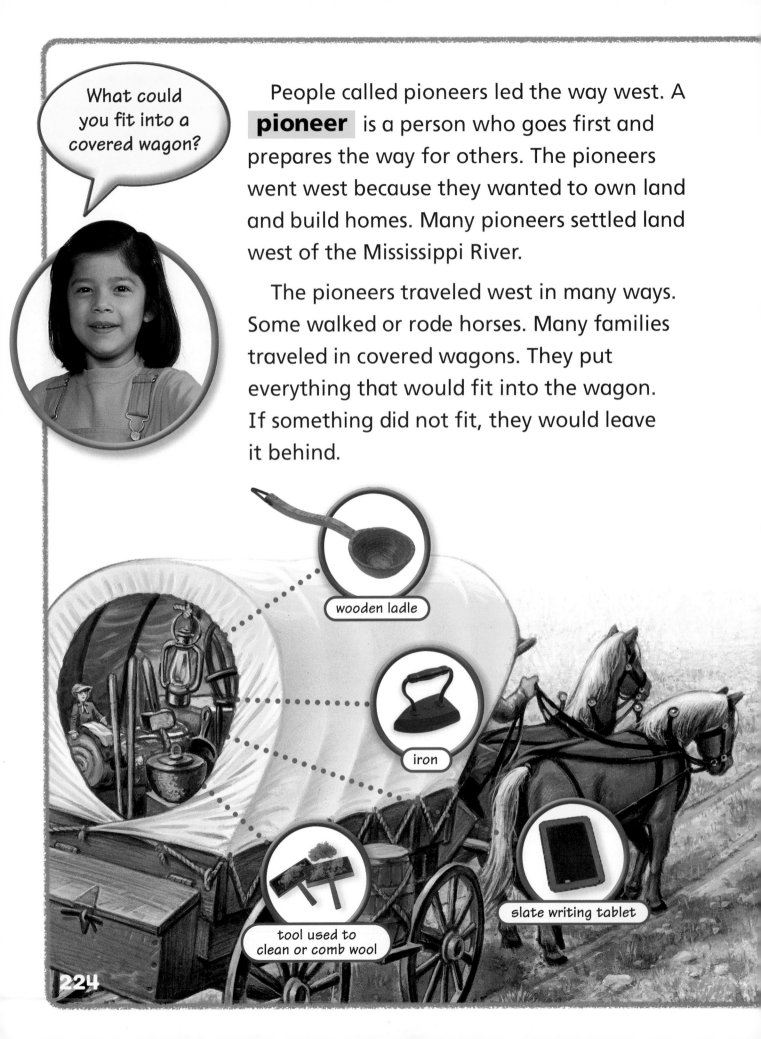

wooden ladle

iron

slate writing tablet

tool used to clean or comb wool

Oregon Trail

Map Key
- Oregon Trail
- Mississippi River
- Rocky Mountains
- Present-day United States borders

Fort Vancouver

Independence

Many pioneers followed the Oregon Trail to the West. The trail was long and hard. The pioneers traveled during rain, wind, and snowstorms. They crossed deserts. They even had to cross the Rocky Mountains.

What did you learn

1. Tell three ways that you learned about Lewis and Clark.

2. Find the Mississippi River on the map. Now find the Rocky Mountains. Which is farther west?

3. **Think and Share** Suppose you were a **pioneer** following the Oregon Trail to the West. Tell what happened **first**, **next**, and **last** on your long trip.

Read a Time Line

I've learned a lot about how our country grew. I made a time line to show some things that happened on the trip Lewis and Clark made. A **time line** shows the order in which things happened.

My Lewis and Clark Time Line

Lewis and Clark began their trip.

Lewis and Clark celebrated Independence Day.

May   **June**   **July**

226

Try it!

1. What month did Lewis and Clark begin their trip?

2. What happened in November?

3. **On Your Own** Make a **time line** that shows how you have grown. Draw pictures of you as a baby, a toddler, and a second grader.

Lewis and Clark saw animals they had never seen before.

Lewis and Clark met Sacagawea.

ugust   September   October   November

Westward Ho!

Many more people wanted to come to the West. Trains were a faster way to travel than covered wagons. Trains were needed so that communities in the West could get supplies they needed.

There were many railroads in the East, but few in the West. The country needed a railroad that could link the East Coast to the West Coast.

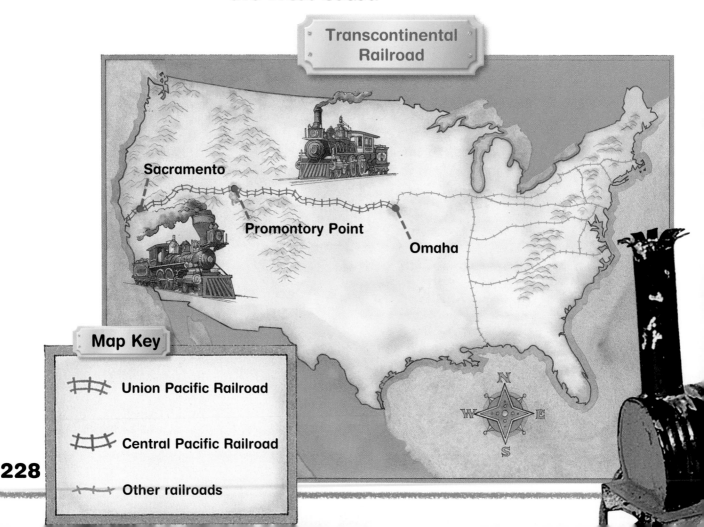

Transcontinental Railroad

Sacramento

Promontory Point

Omaha

Map Key

╫╫╫ Union Pacific Railroad

╫╫╫ Central Pacific Railroad

╫╫╫ Other railroads

228

Two groups built the western part of the railroad. One group started near Omaha, Nebraska. The other group started in Sacramento, California. The two groups met and joined the railroad tracks at Promontory Point in present-day Utah. It took seven years to build this railroad.

Then

Today, high-speed trains link some cities. These trains have a rounded shape and weigh less than older trains. They run with help from computers. High-speed trains can move people very quickly from one city to another.

Now

Hands-on History

Write about how transportation has changed since the pioneers traveled out west. Draw two pictures that show transportation in the past and in the present.

We Remember Americans

As the country grew, not all people were free. Some people were taken from their homes in Africa. They were made to come to America in ships and sold into slavery. Slavery is being owned and having to work for someone else.

Some slaves worked in factories or as servants in homes. Many worked outdoors on small farms or plantations. They raised crops like cotton and sugar. Slaves did not get paid for their hard work.

Slaves working on a Virginia plantation

Some African Americans tried to escape, or run away. Harriet Tubman was a person who escaped to freedom. Later, she led hundreds of other slaves, including her family, to freedom. Harriet Tubman is remembered for her courage.

Frederick Douglass also escaped from slavery. He then wrote a book about his life as a slave. He started a newspaper for African Americans. He is also remembered as a great speaker.

Harriet
Tubman

Frederick
Douglass

Many people thought slavery was wrong. Many others did not. After Abraham Lincoln became President, there was a terrible war in the United States. It was called the Civil War.

Slavery was one of the reasons that the Civil War began. Americans fought Americans in this war. After the Civil War ended, slavery was against the law. President Lincoln helped to end slavery in the United States.

Slavery ended, but African Americans were still not treated fairly. It was difficult for some African Americans to vote or serve in government. Black people were treated differently because of the color of their skin.

A painting titled *The Peace Makers*

Abraham Lincoln

More than 50 years ago, black people were not allowed to play professional sports with white people. Jackie Robinson was the first black player in modern major league baseball. He became a member of the Brooklyn Dodgers. Jackie Robinson said, "The right of every American to first-class citizenship is the most important issue of our time."

Jackie Robinson

Brooklyn Dodgers, 1947

What did you learn?

1. How did Harriet Tubman show courage?

2. What was the name of the war in which Americans fought Americans?

3. **Think and Share** Make a poster showing why Abraham Lincoln was an important leader.

Meet Sojourner Truth

1797–1883

Abolitionist and Suffragist

Sojourner Truth spoke out against slavery. She was once a slave like Harriet Tubman and Frederick Douglass.

When Sojourner Truth was born, she was named Isabella Baumfree. She was a slave until she was about 30 years old. She then changed her name to Sojourner Truth. *Sojourner* means "traveler." She traveled around the country speaking out for the rights of African Americans. She spoke out against slavery. Although she had not learned to read or write, she was a good speaker. President Abraham Lincoln knew of her speeches and invited her to the White House.

Sojourner Truth was born in Ulster County, New York.

Sojourner Truth wanted people to have better lives. When people were freed from slavery, she helped them find new places to live. She gathered supplies for African American soldiers during the Civil War.

Sojourner Truth also spoke out for women's rights. She believed that women should have the right to vote. She spoke at many meetings that supported the women's rights movement.

Sojourner Truth and Abraham Lincoln

Think and Share

Do you think Sojourner Truth chose a good name for herself? Why or why not?

For more information, go online to *Meet the People* at **www.sfsocialstudies.com.**

Follow the Drinkin' Gourd

Some slaves followed the North Star as they fled to freedom. They located the North Star by using the stars of the Big Dipper. They thought the Big Dipper looked like a drinking gourd.

Vocabulary Review

explorer

pioneer

colonist

shelter

tradition

Choose a word to go with each clue.

1. a person who goes first and prepares the way for others

2. a place where people live

3. a person who lives in a colony

4. something that is done a certain way for many years

5. a person who travels to a new place to learn about it

★ ★ ★ ★ ★ ★ ★ ★

 Which word completes each sentence?

1. A place that is settled by people from another country is a _____.

   a. independence   **b.** shelter

   c. colony   **d.** tradition

2. To be free from other people or places is _____.

   a. independence   **b.** pioneer

   c. colony   **d.** tradition

Skills Review

Put Things in Order

Tell what you did today. Use the words **first, next,** and **last** to tell the order in which things happened.

Map and Globe Skills
Use a Map Scale

Look at the map. Use a strip of paper and the map scale to answer the questions.

Test Talk

Use the map to help you find the answers.

1. About how far away is Mara's home from the museum?

2. About how far is the museum from the statue?

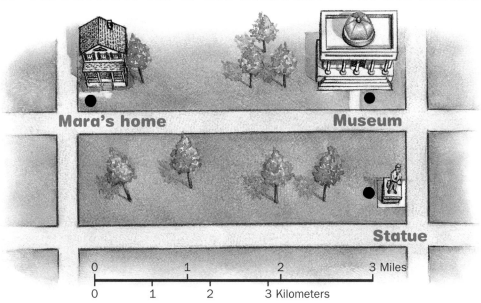

Mara's home   Museum

Statue

```
0        1        2      3 Miles
0    1    2    3 Kilometers
```

Skills Review

Read a Time Line

This is a time line that shows some holidays Americans celebrate. Look at the time line to answer these questions.

1. What month do we celebrate Flag Day?

2. What holiday is celebrated in May?

3. What holiday is last on this time line?

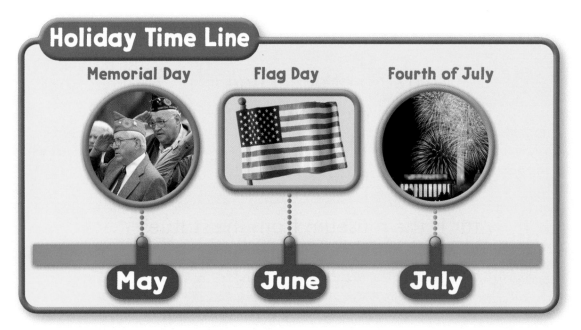

Holiday Time Line

Memorial Day   Flag Day   Fourth of July

May   June   July

Skills on Your Own

Make a celebration time line of your own. Fill in other holidays that you celebrate. Fill in your birthday. Draw pictures above your time line to show each special day.

What did you learn?

1. What resources did the Native Americans use to make their food, clothing, and shelters?

2. Why were many of the colonists willing to fight England?

3. Why did the pioneers move west?

4. **Write and Share** Tell what you would do if you were a pioneer packing your covered wagon for your trip out west. Use the words **first, next,** and **last** to tell the order in which things would happen.

Read About America's History

Look for books like these in the library.

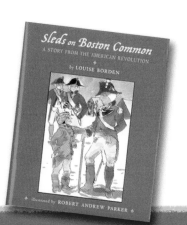

Do an Interview

Here's your chance to talk to a person from the past.

1 **Choose** a person, such as an explorer, a leader, or pioneer.

2 **Prepare** a list of questions to ask and the answers.

3 **Choose** who will play this person and who will play a news reporter.

4 **Present** the interview to your class.

Internet Activity

Go to www.sfsocialstudies.com/activities to learn more about our country long ago.

242

People and Places in History

Why is it important to study people and places from the past?

243

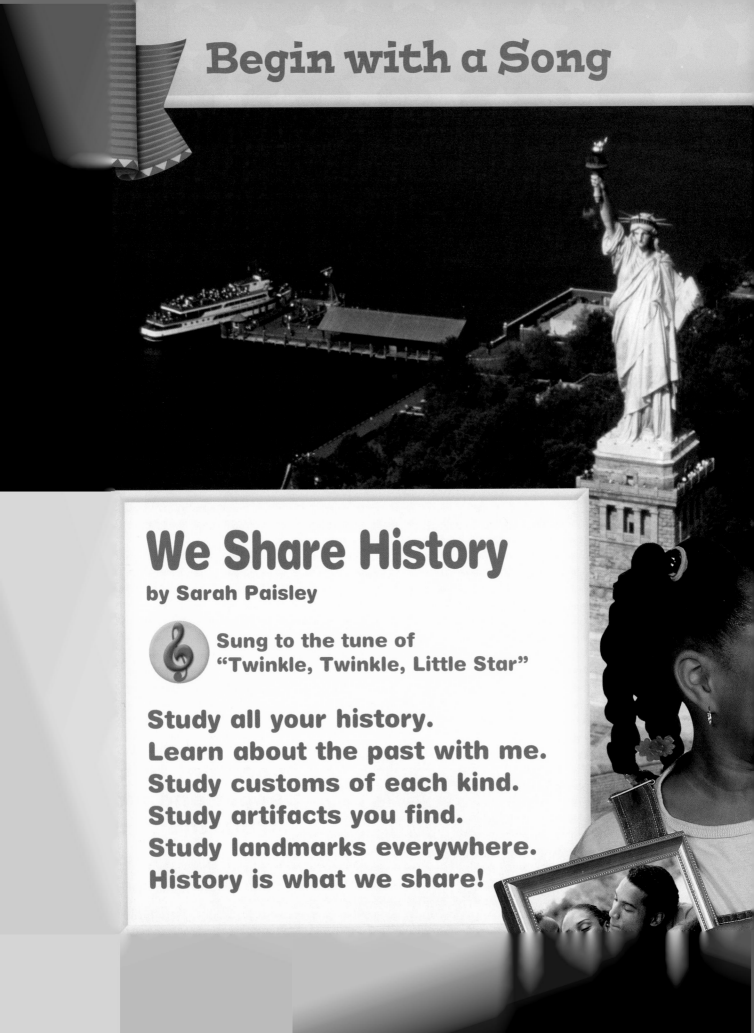

Begin with a Song

We Share History

by Sarah Paisley

Sung to the tune of
"Twinkle, Twinkle, Little Star"

Study all your history.
Learn about the past with me.
Study customs of each kind.
Study artifacts you find.
Study landmarks everywhere.
History is what we share!

245

immigrant

holiday

custom

landmark

Heritage Festival

Artifacts   Inventions

Sign up for the 4th of July Parade

artifact

invention

communication

247

Michael's Family History

Target Skill

Recall and Retell

I wrote a story about my family. Read my story to find out what it is about.

Hi! I'm Michael.

My Family History

My family has a history, or story of the past. I was born in the United States. My parents and grandparents were born here too. My great-grandparents were born in a small town in Germany.

My great-grandparents came to America in 1920, more than 80 years ago! They went to live in Detroit, Michigan. My great-grandpa bought his own bakery. My grandpa and dad now run the bakery. Someday I hope to run the bakery too.

Recalling is thinking about something you have read or heard. **Retelling** is putting it into your own words. Think about Michael's family history. Tell the story in your own words.

This is a picture of my grandpa, my dad, and me.

Try it!

Fold a piece of paper in half from side to side. Now fold it from side to side again. Open your paper and draw four things that happened in "My Family History." Draw them in the order they happened. Use your pictures to **retell** the story of Michael's family.

Lesson 1

Family History

My great-grandparents came to America on a ship. The arrow on the map shows the route they took. Their long journey took them across the Atlantic Ocean.

The first thing they saw when they came into New York Harbor was the Statue of Liberty. To them, it stood for hope and freedom. Many immigrants, like my great-grandparents, came to America in search of a better life. An **immigrant** is a person who settles in a new country.

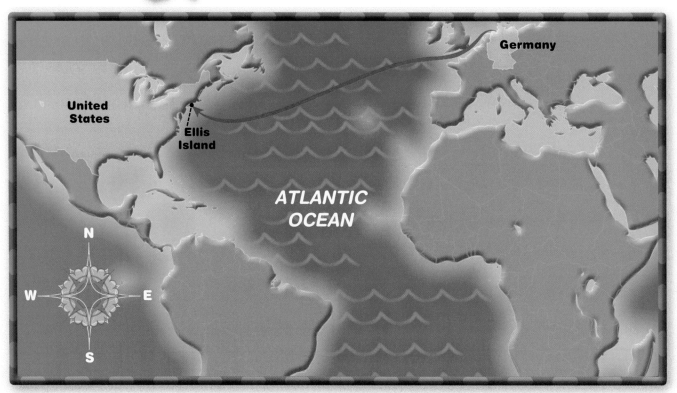

Germany

United States

Ellis Island

ATLANTIC OCEAN

N W E S

Stop.

250

My great-grandparents arrived at Ellis Island, located in New York Harbor. They were checked by a doctor. They had to prove they were healthy and able to work hard.

Immigrants on Ellis Island were asked many questions. *Why do you want to live here? Is someone waiting for you?*

My great-grandmother had a brother living in Detroit, Michigan. When my great-grandparents left Ellis Island, they traveled by train from New York City to Detroit.

Immigrants stand in line at Ellis Island.

Ellis Island

Chinese immigrants

My friend, Amy, had ancestors who were immigrants too. They came to America from China. They traveled from China to San Francisco, California. What ocean did they travel across?

Many immigrants from Asia stopped at Angel Island. Angel Island is an island in the San Francisco Bay. Some immigrants had to live on Angel Island before they could enter the United States.

Angel Island

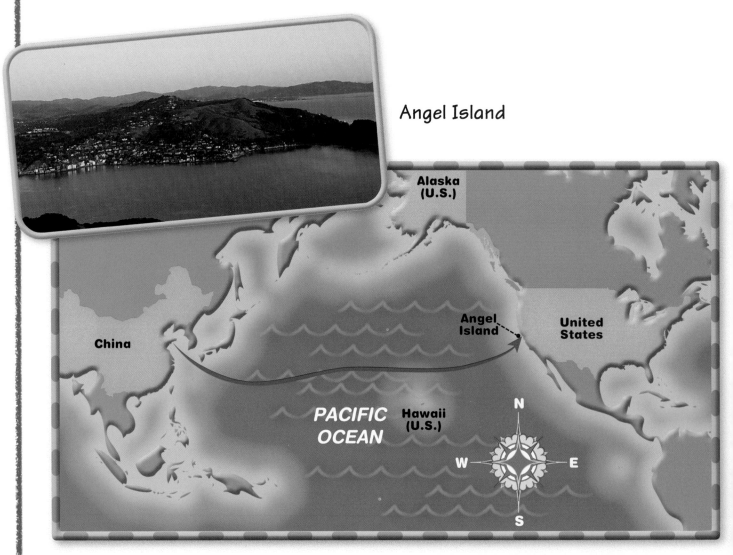

Alaska (U.S.)

China

Angel Island

United States

PACIFIC OCEAN

Hawaii (U.S.)

N

W   E

S

Today, Ellis Island and Angel Island have museums you can visit. My family visited Ellis Island last summer. We saw my great-grandparents' names on the American Immigrant Wall of Honor. This wall honors immigrants who have come to America from around the world. There are many names on the wall.

What did you learn ?

1. Tell how Ellis Island and Angel Island are important to the history of America.

2. What does the Statue of Liberty stand for?

3. **Think and Share**
Recall the story about Amy's **immigrant** ancestors. Use your own words to **retell** about them.

Ellen Ochoa trained at the Johnson Space Center in Houston, Texas.

Ellen Ochoa

It took courage for immigrants to come to America. Many didn't speak English or know anyone in this country. For Ellen Ochoa, it takes a different kind of courage to do her job!

Ellen Ochoa became the first Hispanic female astronaut in NASA's Space Program. She has been on three space flights and is looking forward to more. She thinks it is very important for people to explore space. It takes courage and a sense of adventure to explore new places.

BUILDING
CITIZENSHIP
Caring
Respect
Responsibility
Fairness
Honesty
★ Courage

As a student, Ellen Ochoa always liked school. As an astronaut, she learns new things every day just as she did in school. She thinks that being an astronaut is very exciting!

Ellen Ochoa helped develop computer systems to explore space. She also helped invent better ways for people to look closely at objects in space. She was a crew member on a space flight that delivered supplies to the International Space Station. Ellen Ochoa dreams of helping build a space station. She has received many awards from NASA for her service.

★ Courage in Action ★

Why does it take courage to explore new places?

Dr. Ochoa aboard Discovery Space Shuttle

255

People Celebrate

My family and I celebrate many holidays. A **holiday** is a special day. Many people do not work on holidays. Some holidays are national holidays, or days that are important to all Americans. Look at the time line. How do you celebrate these national holidays?

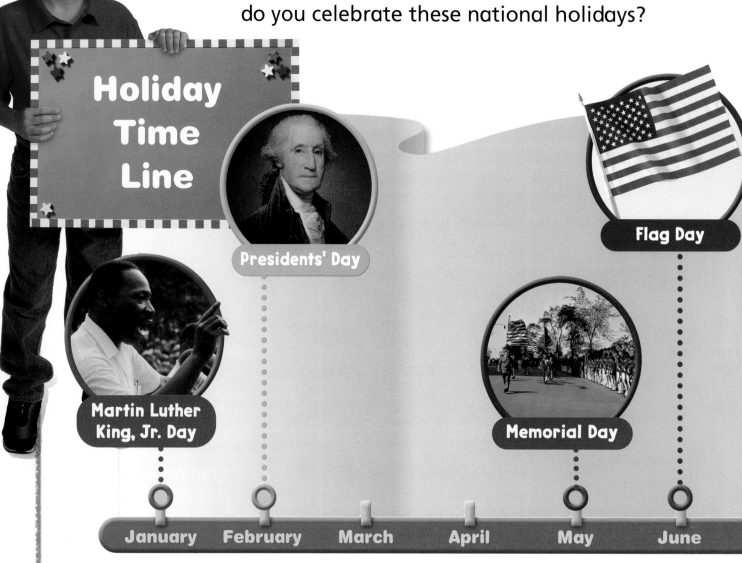

Holiday
Time
Line

Presidents' Day

Flag Day

Memorial Day

Martin Luther
King, Jr. Day

| January | February | March | April | May | June |

256

Two holidays, Memorial Day and Veterans Day, remember people who fought in wars for our country. Memorial Day honors all United States citizens who have died in war. On Veterans Day, we remember all of the men and women who have fought to keep our country free. In which months are these holidays celebrated?

In many communities, it is a custom to march in parades on these holidays. A **custom** is a special way that a group does something. It is also a custom to give speeches on these holidays.

Veterans Day

Labor Day

Columbus Day

Thanksgiving

Independence Day

July   August   September   October   November   December

Breaking a piñata

Many communities celebrate other holidays. Cinco de Mayo, or May 5, is an important holiday for Mexican Americans. It celebrates the courage of the Mexican people. On this day, in 1862, there was a battle in Mexico. A small Mexican Army won a battle against a much larger French Army.

Today, people celebrate this holiday in many ways. It is a custom to have fiestas, or feasts. Foods like warm tortillas, tamales, and rice are served. Children break piñatas filled with toys and candies.

Some African Americans celebrate each June 19. It is called Juneteenth. In 1865, this day marked the end of slavery in Texas.

On Juneteenth, it is a custom that families get together. They may tell stories about their ancestors. Some families have picnics and play baseball. Other people sing songs and give thanks for freedom.

Celebrating Juneteenth then and now

What did you learn?

1. What are three national **holidays** that Americans celebrate?

2. How do you celebrate Memorial Day in your state or community?

3. **Think and Share** Draw a picture of a **holiday** **custom** that you share with your family. Write a poem about your picture.

Spring

Springtime festivals celebrate new life, energy, and growth. For many children, these are happy, colorful festivals with flowers, music, and dancing.

Chinese New Year starts on the first day of the Chinese calendar and lasts for 15 days. Man Po and her family feast, visit friends, and watch colorful street parades.

The N'cwala ceremony is held each February to celebrate the harvest. Groups of dancers perform their warrior dance. M'sangombe is the youngest dancer in his group.

Fête des Mères is celebrated on the last Sunday in May. Matilde calls this day Mommy's Festival. Matilde brings her mother breakfast in bed and recites the poem she has learned.

Hina Matsuri is celebrated March 3. This is a day dedicated to dolls. During the festival, Sayo displays her dolls in the best room of the house.

Man Po from Hong Kong

M'sangombe from Zambia

Matilde from France

Sayo from Japan

Sophie from England

The children in Sophie's village celebrate May Day on May 1. They listen to music, pick spring flowers, and dance around a maypole.

Read a Calendar

A **calendar** is a kind of chart that shows days, weeks, months, and years. A calendar helps us tell about and measure time. It also helps us remember important days.

May

Sunday	Monday	Tuesday	Wednesday	Thursday
				1
4	5	6	7	8
11 Mother's Day	12	13	14	15
18	19	20	21	22
25	26 Memorial Day	27	28	29

262

Look at Michael's calendar for May. How many days are in this month? Find the day Michael celebrates his birthday. On which day of the week is Mother's Day?

Friday	Saturday
2	3 Michael's Birthday
9	10
16	17
23	24
30	31

Try it!

1. What national holiday do we celebrate in May?

2. On what four days does Michael have soccer games?

3. **On Your Own** Draw your own calendar for this month. Put important dates on it.

Landmarks in Our Country

My dad is taking me on a trip to Chicago. We will see the Cubs play baseball! The Cubs play at Wrigley Field. This ballpark is a landmark in the community. A **landmark** is a building or place that is important or interesting.

Wrigley Field was built more than 85 years ago. It is one of the oldest ballparks in our country. Look at these pictures. How has Wrigley Field changed over time?

Then

Now

Every state has important landmarks.
What are some landmarks in your state?

The Gateway Arch is at the edge of the Mississippi River in Missouri. It reminds people that America grew much larger when pioneers moved out west.

Castillo de San Marcos in Florida is one of the oldest forts in the United States. It has thick walls made of shell stone. The fort was built long ago to protect the Spanish colony of St. Augustine.

In 1836, Texas was fighting to be free from Mexico's rule. For 13 days, a small group of Texans defended the Alamo against thousands of Mexican soldiers. The Alamo is a famous landmark to Texans.

Our country has national landmarks too. National landmarks are important because they help us learn about the history of our country.

Mount Rushmore is a landmark in the Black Hills of South Dakota. The faces of Presidents George Washington, Thomas Jefferson, Theodore Roosevelt, and Abraham Lincoln are carved into the side of a mountain.

The Statue of Liberty stands for liberty, or freedom. The Statue of Liberty was a gift from the people of France to the people of the United States.

The United States Capitol is located in Washington, D.C. Congress works in the Capitol building.

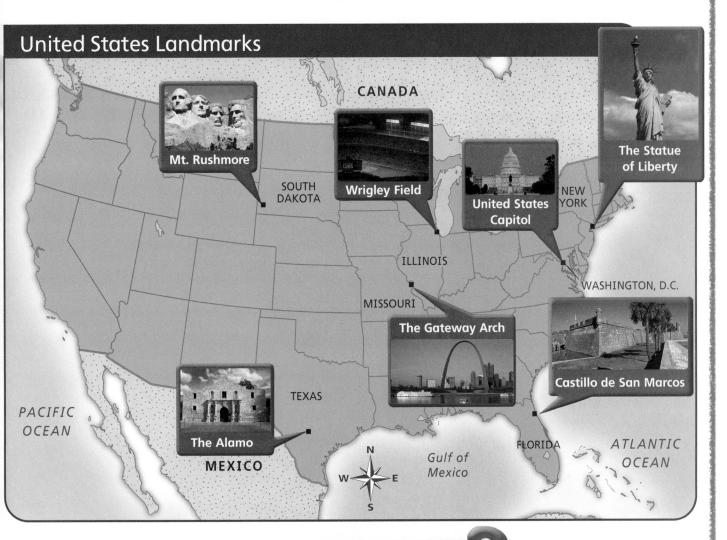

United States Landmarks

Mt. Rushmore

CANADA

Wrigley Field

United States Capitol

The Statue of Liberty

SOUTH DAKOTA

NEW YORK

ILLINOIS

WASHINGTON, D.C.

MISSOURI

The Gateway Arch

Castillo de San Marcos

PACIFIC OCEAN

The Alamo

TEXAS

MEXICO

N
W   E
S

Gulf of Mexico

FLORIDA

ATLANTIC OCEAN

What did you learn?

1. How does the Mount Rushmore **landmark** honor the history of our country?

2. Look at the map. Tell where the United States Capitol is located.

3. **Think and Share** Draw a picture of a statue or other landmark in your community. Explain why it is important.

Meet
Ieoh Ming Pei

1917–
Architect

I. (Ieoh) M. (Ming) Pei has designed landmark buildings in the United States and around the world.

I. M. Pei was born in China. When he was a teenager, he was fascinated by the tall modern buildings he saw. When he was 18 years old, he came to the United States. He wanted to become an architect. An architect is a person who designs buildings.

Ieoh Ming Pei was born in Canton (now Guangzhou), China.

After he finished school, I. M. Pei worked for other architects. He also taught students about how to design buildings. During this time, he became a citizen of the United States. Then he started his own architecture business. He designed projects in the United States and around the world.

I. M. Pei has designed libraries, office buildings, airline terminals, hotels, and schools, but his favorite work is designing museums. He enjoys learning about places and people so he can design buildings that fit the special needs of each. He likes to design buildings that people enjoy visiting.

East Wing, National Gallery of Art, Washington, D.C.

Think and Share

How has I. M. Pei made the world a more beautiful place to live?

For more information, go online to *Meet the People* at **www.sfsocialstudies.com**.

Landmarks Around the World

Take a look at two countries that have important landmarks. Our first stop is the country of Egypt on the continent of Africa. Find Egypt on the globe.

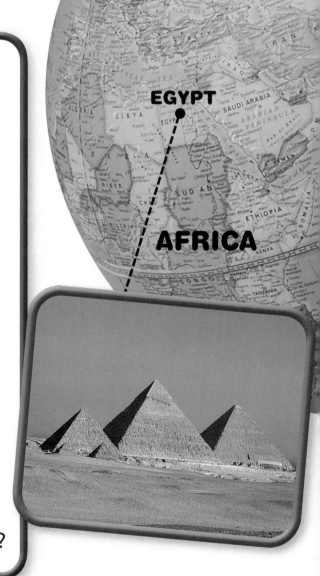

EGYPT

AFRICA

In ancient Egypt, kings and queens were buried inside stone pyramids. A pyramid has four triangular sides that come to a point at the top.

It took thousands of people to build one pyramid. Each block of stone weighed more than your family's car! Some pyramids are so large that they could cover several football fields.

Today, we still wonder how the Egyptians built the pyramids without using modern machines. How do you think they built them?

ASIA

CHINA

Our next stop is the country of China. Look at the globe. On which continent is China located?

The Great Wall of China was built more than 2,000 years ago. It took about 1 million people to build it! Ancient Chinese states first built walls for protection. Later these walls were joined together and called the Great Wall.

If you put the Great Wall across the United States, from east to west, it would be much longer than our country!

Hands-on History

The pyramids in Egypt and the Great Wall in China are ancient landmarks still standing today. Draw a modern landmark that you think will still be standing thousands of years from now.

4 A Step Back in Time

I am learning about Egypt and China.

Another way to learn about the past is by looking at artifacts. An **artifact** is an object made and used by people.

People from the past left behind many artifacts. These artifacts give us clues about their way of life. What can you tell about how people lived long ago?

Artifacts

Egyptian carved cup

Egyptian ring with horses

Egyptian queen statue

Chinese bronze leopard

Chinese jade figure

Chinese vase

Egypt

The Egyptians had a system of writing called hieroglyphics. They drew pictures and symbols on walls. They also wrote on stone and clay tablets.

Later, the Egyptians made ink and pens. They wrote on papyrus, a thin paper-like material made from tall grass. Our word *paper* comes from the word *papyrus*.

Egyptian hieroglyphics

China

The Chinese had a system of writing too. They wrote symbols called characters on bones, shells, and strips of bamboo. These characters stood for objects and ideas. Today, the Chinese still use characters as their system of writing.

Chinese characters

Nile River

The Egyptians and the Chinese used calendars. An Egyptian calendar measured the seasons. It also measured the rise and fall of the Nile River. The Egyptian calendar had 12 months in one year. Each month had 30 days that added up to 360 days. The Egyptians then added 5 days at the end of the year to make 365 days. How many days do we have in one year?

The Chinese use a calendar based on the phases of the moon. It is called the Chinese Lunar Calendar. *Lunar* means "like the moon." Each lunar year is named after an animal.

Egyptian stone calendar

Chinese calendar

An **invention** is something new that someone makes or thinks of. The Chinese made many inventions. Many of these inventions, such as the wheelbarrow and kite, are still used today.

The ancient Egyptians built obelisks. An obelisk is a huge monument that points toward the sky. The Washington Monument in Washington, D.C., is built in the shape of an obelisk.

Luxor obelisk, Egypt

What did you learn?

1. What do we learn by looking at **artifacts?**

2. What **inventions** have ancient China and Egypt given us that we still use today?

3. **Think and Share** Draw a picture of something today that may someday be an artifact. Write about why you think so.

Read a Diagram

China was once called Cathay. Long ago, a merchant named Marco Polo traveled from Italy to Cathay, or China. He traded goods with other merchants along the way. Marco Polo traveled by water and land. Across land, he traveled in a caravan. A caravan is a traveling group.

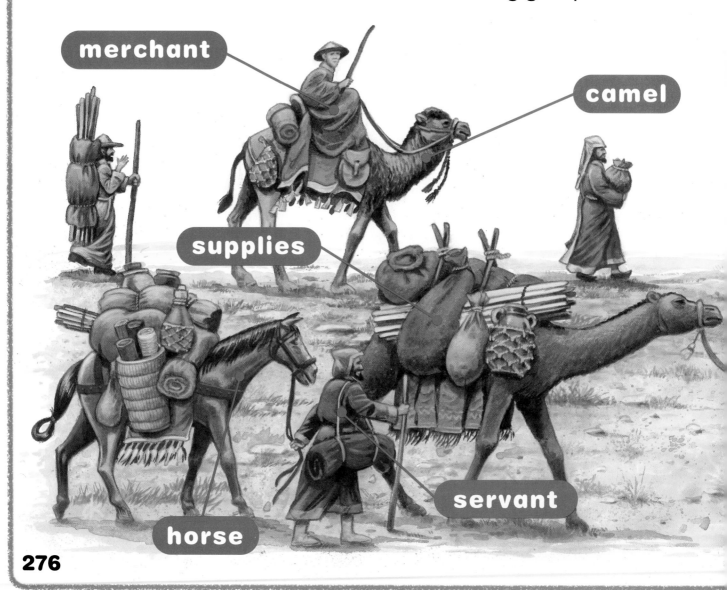

Below is a diagram of a caravan. A **diagram** is a drawing that shows the parts of something. A diagram gives information in a chart or picture instead of sentences. Look at the diagram. What animals are in the caravan?

Marco Polo's route

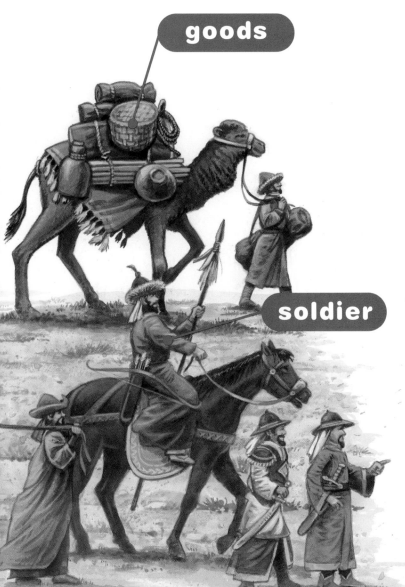

goods

soldier

1. What animal is carrying goods and supplies?

2. What people are traveling in the caravan?

3. **On Your Own** Make a **diagram** of your favorite toy. Label the parts.

277

5 Linking Our World

People share ideas in many ways. Sharing ideas and information with others is **communication.** Communication links people in our world together.

Long ago, people wrote on walls and stone. Today, people use inventions such as the telephone, computer, and fax machine to communicate. What would happen if we didn't have these inventions? How would we communicate with someone in another country?

In class, we learn how important it is to communicate and work together. How are these people communicating?

Some people communicate in other ways. Helen Keller was someone who could not hear or see. She communicated by using a form of sign language. She also learned Braille. Braille is a special way to read and write. Helen Keller helped others who couldn't hear or see. She wrote books about her life.

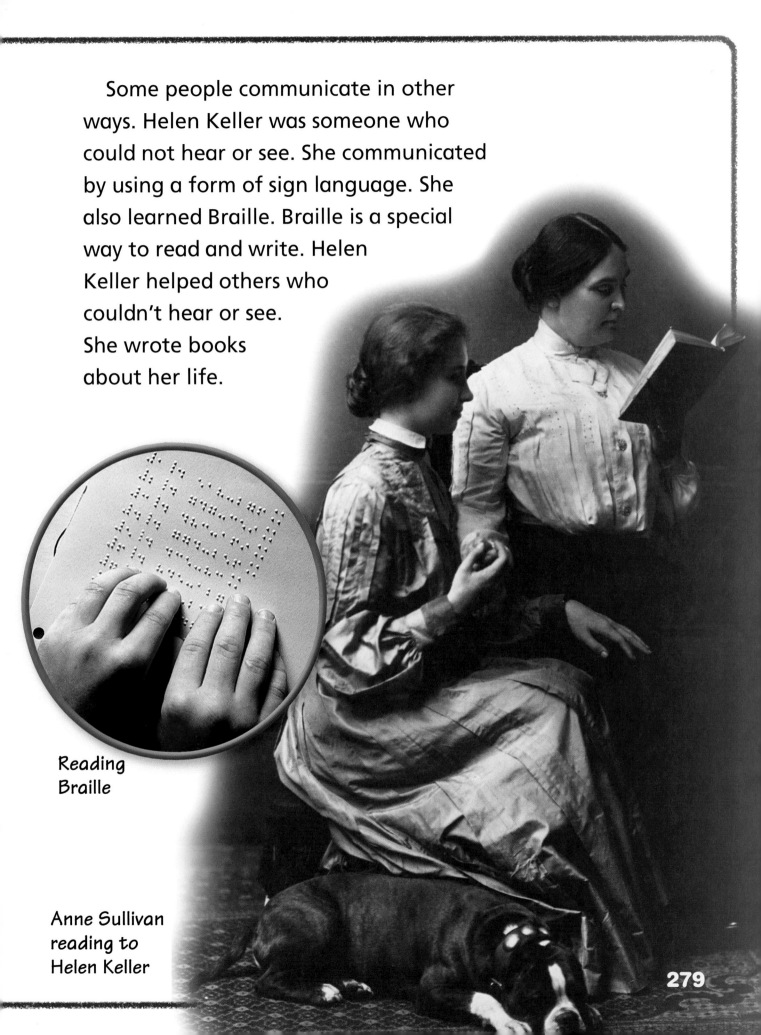

Reading Braille

Anne Sullivan reading to Helen Keller

Henry Ford sitting in his first car

Transportation also links people in our world. In the past, most people traveled by using horses, wagons, and trains.

In 1893, Henry Ford built an engine that used gasoline. A few years later, he built what was called a "horseless carriage." It had a motor on a frame with bicycle wheels. These first cars were very expensive because they were built one by one.

Soon, Henry Ford and his company started building many cars at the same time. They built a less expensive car that more people could buy. It was called the Model T.

Cars today are much different from the Model T. They are safer and more comfortable. Computers help cars of the present run better.

For hundreds of years, inventors experimented with flying machines. Then, in 1903, the Wright brothers made the first successful powered airplane flight.

Amelia Earhart was the first woman to fly alone across the Atlantic Ocean. In 1937, she began a flight around the world. Her plane disappeared. Amelia Earhart and the Wright brothers are remembered each year on National Aviation Day.

Today, many people travel the world by jet. What kind of transportation might link communities in the future?

What did you learn?

1. How have **inventions** changed **communication** and transportation?

2. Why is Amelia Earhart an important person in our country's history?

3. **Think and Share** Make a poster. Show transportation in the past, the present, and the future. Tell about your poster.

Meet
Robert Fulton

1765–1815
Inventor and Artist

Robert Fulton built different kinds of transportation that could travel on or under water.

As a young man, Robert was interested in painting. He was also interested in new inventions.

Robert Fulton was born in Lancaster County, Pennsylvania.

Robert Fulton moved from the United States to France. While in France, he had an idea for a new use for submarines. He built the *Nautilus.* It was a submarine, or boat that could travel underwater. It could even travel under ships! Robert Fulton also planned the building of a steamboat.

Robert Fulton moved back to the United States and began work building a steamboat. He made many improvements to the steamboat over the next few years. In 1807, his boat, called the *Clermont,* was tested on the Hudson River. It was the first steamboat service that moved both people and goods. The *Clermont* traveled from New York City to Albany.

the Nautilus

Fulton Street in New York City is named after this famous inventor. A statue in Statuary Hall, Washington, D.C., also honors Robert Fulton.

Think and Share

How have Americans remembered Robert Fulton?

Fulton Street, New York City

 For more information, go online to *Meet the People* at **www.sfsocialstudies.com.**

An Honest Man

A Chinese Folktale as told by Li Hongling

It is a custom for the Chinese to create stories about their world. Sharing these stories is another way to communicate.

Long ago, there was a valley where ten poor families lived. In the valley was a pool of water. One day many guests came to visit one of the families. It was rare for visitors to come to the valley, so the head of the family welcomed them and decided to have a feast. Because he was a poor man, he did not have enough plates for all of his guests, so he borrowed some from a neighbor.

After the meal, he went to the pool to clean the plates. Suddenly one of the plates slid into the water, and, though he searched and searched, he could not find it. He was very much disturbed by this and sat by the pool feeling very unhappy, trying to figure out what to do.

"Can I help you?" came a soft voice from the water.

The man looked into the water and saw a goldfish. Surprised by what he saw, he said, "Oh, a plate I borrowed from my neighbor slid into the water. How can I return it to him?"

The fish disappeared for a while, then appeared with a golden plate. He asked the man, "Is this plate yours?"

The poor man answered honestly that it was not the plate he had lost, so the fish disappeared again. After a few minutes, the fish came back with another plate, this time a silver one. Again, the poor man told the fish that it was not his plate. The fish disappeared again.

In a short while, the fish returned with the right plate. This time the man said, "Oh, yes. That's the one I'm looking for. Thank you very much!"

And what do you know! Because the man had been so honest, the fish gave him all three plates to take home to his family.

Vocabulary Review

landmark

holiday

artifact

custom

invention

Choose a word from the box to complete each sentence.

1. Giving speeches on Memorial Day is a _____.

2. The Statue of Liberty is a _____.

3. An object that can tell us about the past is an _____.

4. A special day is a _____.

★ ★ ★ ★ ★ ★ ★ ★

Which word completes each sentence?

1. A person who settles in a new country is an _____.

   a. artifact   **b.** immigrant

   c. invention   **d.** landmark

2. Sharing information and ideas is _____.

   a. invention   **c.** communication

   b. custom   **d.** landmark

Skills Review

Recall and Retell

Recall what you read about Helen Keller or another important person. **Retell** the story of that person in your own words.

★ ★ ★ ★ ★ ★ ★ ★

Study Skills

Read a Calendar

Use this calendar to answer the questions.

1. How many days are there in one week?

2. What holiday is celebrated on the fourth Thursday of November?

3. Is Veterans Day before or after Election Day?

			November			
Sunday	Monday	Tuesday	Wednesday	Thursday	Friday	Saturday
						1
2	3	4 **Election Day**	5	6	7	8
9	10	11 **Veterans Day**	12	13	14	15
16	17	18	19	20	21	22
23	24	25	26	27 **Thanksgiving**	28	29
30						

Skills Review
Read a Diagram

Look at the diagram of a bicycle.

1. How many tires are on a bicycle?

2. What does your foot push to make the bicycle move?

3. Where do you sit on the bicycle?

seat

handlebar

pedal

tire

Test Talk

Is your answer complete and correct?

Skills on Your Own

Draw a diagram of a car. Label some of the parts. Write a description of a car.

288

What did you learn?

1. Why do immigrants come to the United States?

2. Explain why many Mexican Americans celebrate Cinco de Mayo.

3. Explain why national landmarks are important?

4. **Think and Share** Think of a new holiday you could add to the calendar. Name your holiday. Tell how you would celebrate this holiday.

Read About People and Places in History

Look for books like these in the library.

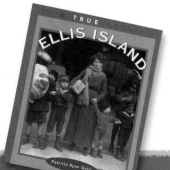

My Hero

Talk about your own hero.

1 **Choose** a person you think is a hero.

2 **Write** why the person is a hero to you.

3 **Draw** a picture of your hero. Draw or make a medal or a ribbon for your hero.

4 **Tell** the class about your hero.

Internet Activity

Go to www.sfsocialstudies.com/activities to learn more about places in history.

Reference Guide

Table of Contents

Atlas
Photograph of the Earth

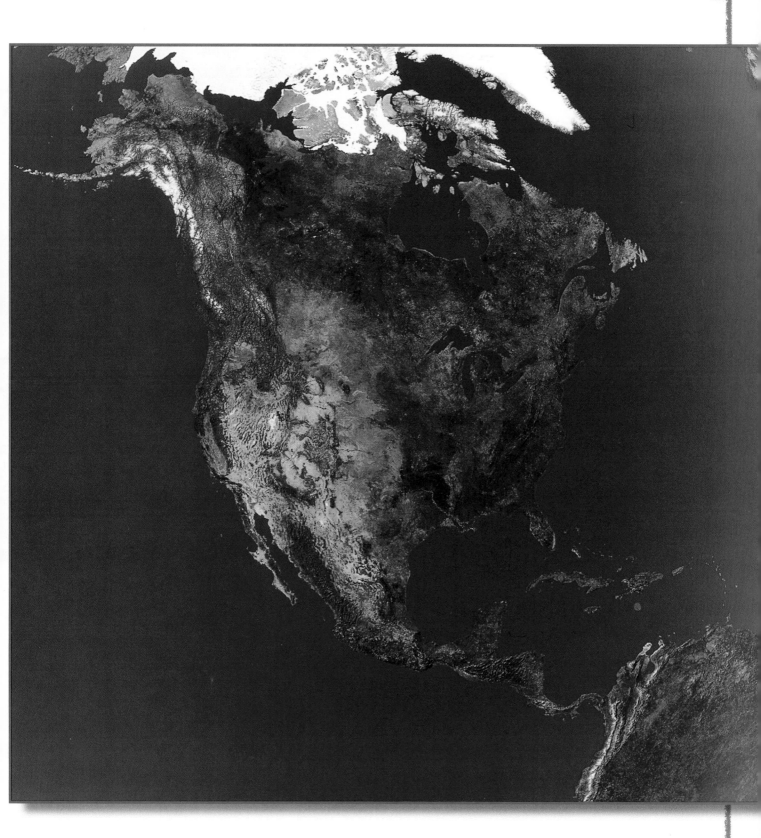

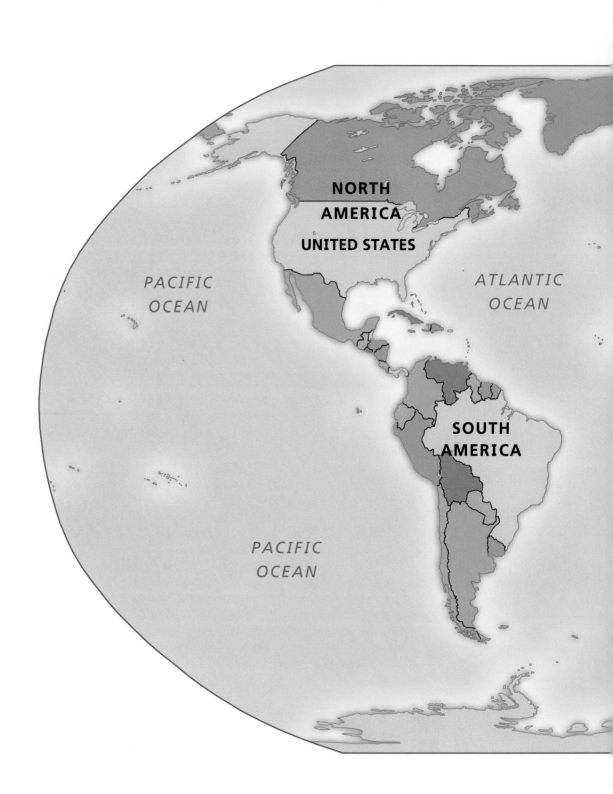

NORTH
AMERICA

UNITED STATES

PACIFIC
OCEAN

ATLANTIC
OCEAN

SOUTH
AMERICA

PACIFIC
OCEAN

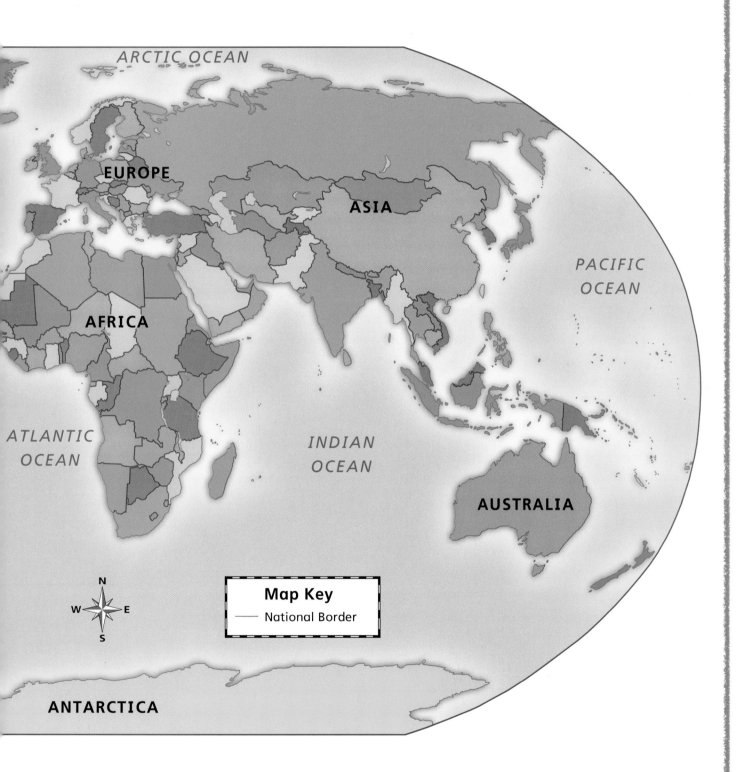

ARCTIC OCEAN

EUROPE

ASIA

PACIFIC
OCEAN

AFRICA

ATLANTIC
OCEAN

INDIAN
OCEAN

AUSTRALIA

N
W   E
S

Map Key
—— National Border

ANTARCTICA

Atlas

Map of the United States of America

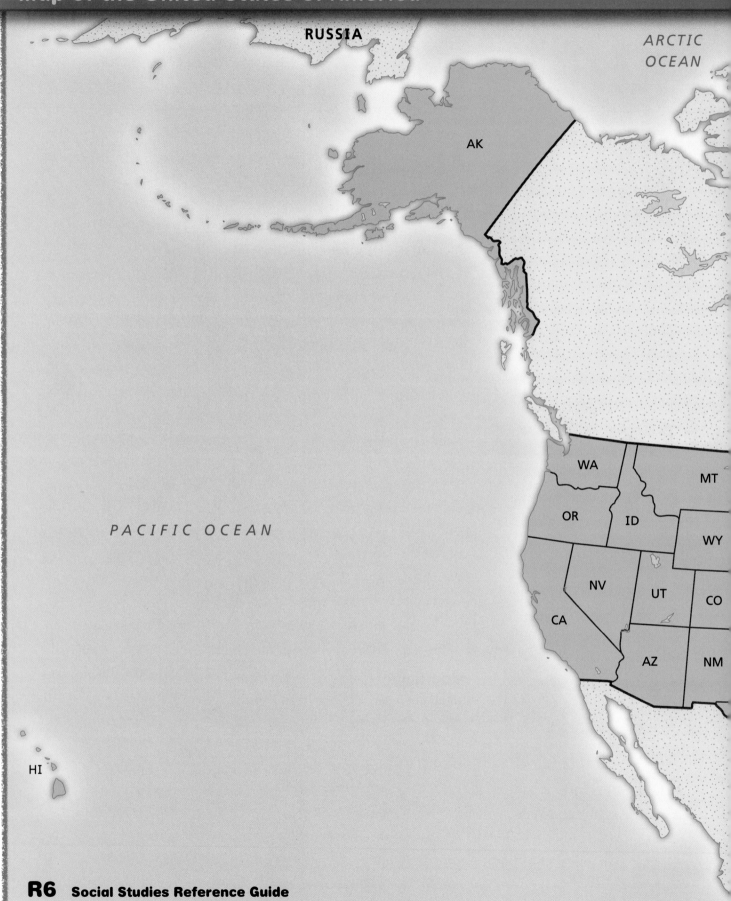

RUSSIA

ARCTIC OCEAN

AK

WA

MT

OR

ID

WY

NV

UT

CO

CA

AZ

NM

PACIFIC OCEAN

HI

State or area	Abbreviation
Alabama	AL
Alaska	AK
Arizona	AZ
Arkansas	AR
California	CA
Colorado	CO
Connecticut	CT
Delaware	DE
District of Columbia	DC
Florida	FL
Georgia	GA
Hawaii	HI
Idaho	ID
Illinois	IL
Indiana	IN
Iowa	IA
Kansas	KS
Kentucky	KY
Louisiana	LA
Maine	ME
Maryland	MD
Massachusetts	MA
Michigan	MI
Minnesota	MN
Mississippi	MS
Missouri	MO
Montana	MT
Nebraska	NE
Nevada	NV
New Hampshire	NH
New Jersey	NJ
New Mexico	NM
New York	NY
North Carolina	NC
North Dakota	ND
Ohio	OH
Oklahoma	OK
Oregon	OR
Pennsylvania	PA
Rhode Island	RI
South Carolina	SC
South Dakota	SD
Tennessee	TN
Texas	TX
Utah	UT
Vermont	VT
Virginia	VA
Washington	WA
West Virginia	WV
Wisconsin	WI
Wyoming	WY

Atlas
Map of Our Fifty States

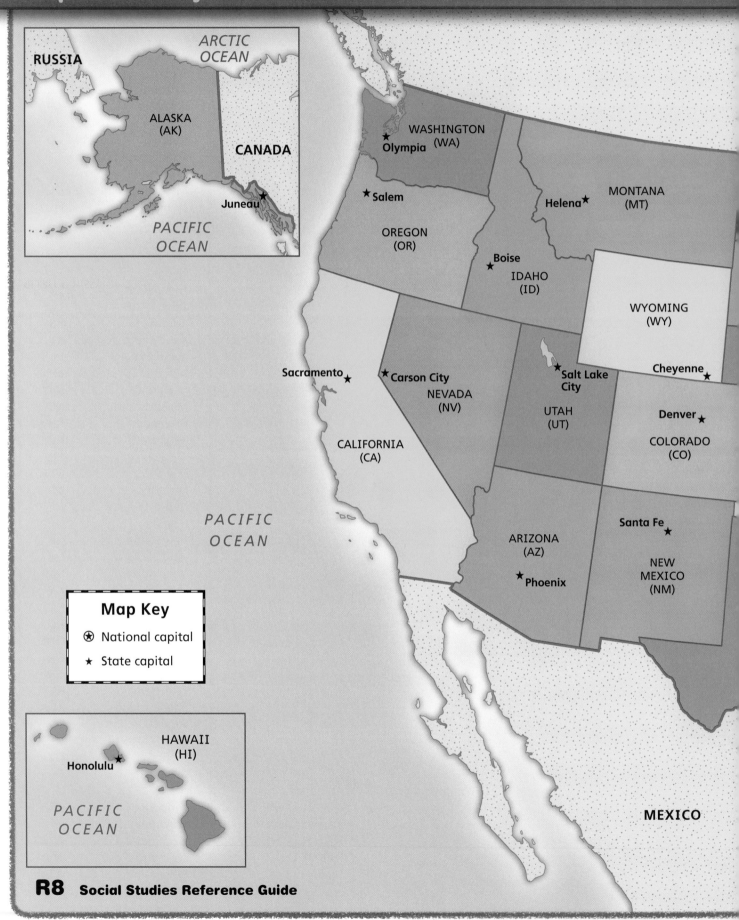

RUSSIA

ARCTIC OCEAN

ALASKA (AK)

CANADA

Juneau

PACIFIC OCEAN

WASHINGTON (WA)
Olympia

Salem

OREGON (OR)

Helena

MONTANA (MT)

Boise

IDAHO (ID)

WYOMING (WY)

Cheyenne

Sacramento

Carson City

NEVADA (NV)

Salt Lake City

UTAH (UT)

Denver

COLORADO (CO)

CALIFORNIA (CA)

PACIFIC OCEAN

Santa Fe

ARIZONA (AZ)

NEW MEXICO (NM)

Phoenix

Map Key
⊛ National capital
★ State capital

HAWAII (HI)
Honolulu

PACIFIC OCEAN

MEXICO

CANADA

NORTH DAKOTA
(ND)
★ Bismarck

MINNESOTA
(MN)

Lake Superior

NEW HAMPSHIRE (NH)
VERMONT (VT)

MAINE
(ME)
★ Augusta

SOUTH DAKOTA
(SD)
★ Pierre

St. Paul ★

WISCONSIN
(WI)

Lake Michigan

Lake Huron

MICHIGAN
(MI)

Montpelier
★

Concord
★

MASSACHUSETTS
(MA)

Madison
★

Lake Ontario

Albany
★

Boston
★

Lake Erie

NEW YORK
(NY)

★ Providence

Hartford ★

RHODE ISLAND
(RI)

NEBRASKA
(NE)

IOWA
(IA)

Lansing ★

CONNECTICUT
(CT)

PENNSYLVANIA
(PA)

★ Trenton

NEW JERSEY (NJ)

Lincoln ★

Des Moines
★

ILLINOIS
(IL)

INDIANA
(IN)

OHIO
(OH)

Harrisburg ★

DELAWARE (DE)

Topeka
★

KANSAS
(KS)

MISSOURI
(MO)

Springfield
★

Indianapolis
★

Columbus
★

Annapolis
★

★ Dover

MARYLAND (MD)

WEST
VIRGINIA
(WV)

Richmond
★

Washington, D.C.

Jefferson
City ★

Charleston
★

VIRGINIA
(VA)

OKLAHOMA
(OK)

★ Oklahoma
City

ARKANSAS
(AR)

Frankfort
★

KENTUCKY
(KY)

Raleigh
★

Knoxville
★

NORTH CAROLINA
(NC)

TENNESSEE
(TN)

Little
Rock ★

Columbia
★

SOUTH
CAROLINA
(SC)

ALABAMA
(AL)

Atlanta
★

MISSISSIPPI
(MS)

GEORGIA
(GA)

TEXAS
(TX)

Jackson
★

Montgomery
★

ATLANTIC
OCEAN

LOUISIANA
(LA)

Tallahassee
★

★ Austin

Baton
Rouge ★

FLORIDA
(FL)

Gulf of Mexico

N
W   E
S

BAHAMAS

CUBA

Geography Terms

forest
large area of land where
many trees grow

hill
rounded land higher than the
land around it

island
land with water all around it

lake
large body of water with land
all or nearly all around it

mountain
highest land on Earth

ocean
a huge body of salt water

ocean

island

lake

hill

peninsula
land that is almost surrounded by water

plain
large, mostly flat, area of land

river
large stream of water leading to a lake, other river, or ocean

valley
low land between mountains or hills

mountain

valley

plain

river

forest

peninsula

Picture Glossary

ancestor
A person in my family who lived before I was born. My great-grandmother is my **ancestor.** (page 68)

artifact
An object made and used by people. We can learn about the past when we look at an **artifact.** (page 272)

bar graph
A picture that helps you compare groups. This **bar graph** shows foods that Josh's class likes. (page 80)

barter
To trade goods or services for other goods or services without using money. People can **barter** to get what they need. (page 138)

calendar
A chart that shows days, weeks, months, and years. A **calendar** helps us remember important days. (page 262)

capital

The city where the leaders of a state or country work. Washington, D.C., is the **capital** of the United States. (page 33)

citizen

A member of a community, state, and country. I am a **citizen** of the United States of America. (page 155)

colonist

A person who lives in a colony. A **colonist** in Jamestown had to work hard. (page 211)

colony

A place that is settled by people from another country. Virginia was an English **colony.** (page 210)

communication

Sharing ideas and information with others. The telephone is used for **communication.** (page 278)

community

A place that is made up of many neighborhoods. There are many stores in my **community.** (page 16)

compass rose

Shows directions on a map. He saw the directions on the **compass rose.** (page 124)

Congress

The part of government that writes and votes on laws for all of our states. I hope to be elected to **Congress** someday. (page 167)

conservation

The care and protection of land, water, plants, and animals. Park rangers teach people about **conservation.** (page 82)

consumer

Someone who buys and uses goods. A **consumer** buys goods at the store. (page 71)

crop

A kind of plant that people grow and use. Corn is a **crop** that provides food. (page 78)

custom

A special way that a group does something. It is a **custom** to celebrate some holidays by having a parade. (page 257)

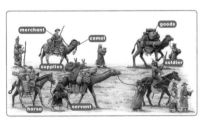

D

diagram

A drawing that shows the parts of something and gives information. We look at the **diagram** to learn more about a caravan. (page 277)

explorer

A person who travels to a new place to learn about it. Meriwether Lewis was an **explorer.** (page 210)

factory

A building where people produce or process goods. Juice is bottled in this **factory.** (page 120)

freedom

Every citizen's right to make choices. The Liberty Bell is a symbol of **freedom.** (page 180)

geography

The study of the Earth and the ways people use it. The globe helps me learn about **geography.** (page 56)

goods

Things that people make or grow. Many kinds of **goods** are sold in stores. (page 104)

government

A group of people who work together to run a city, state, or country. Our **government** makes laws to help keep us safe. (page 154)

governor

The leader of a state's government. The **governor** came to our city. (page 160)

grid

A pattern of lines that form squares. The **grid** helps me find places on the map. (page 185)

history

Tells the story of people and places from the past. Pictures of people can tell you about **history.** (page 22)

holiday

A special day. Our favorite **holiday** is Independence Day. (page 256)

immigrant

A person who settles in a new country. My grandfather was an **immigrant** to our country. (page 250)

income

Money that someone earns. Some of my family's **income** is used to buy shoes. (page 104)

independence

To be free from other people or places. The colonists wanted **independence** from England. (page 217)

invention

Something new that someone makes or thinks of. The wheelbarrow is an **invention** many people use. (page 275)

landform

Different shapes on the surface of the earth. A mountain is a kind of **landform.** (page 56)

landmark

A building or place that is important or interesting. Mount Rushmore is a **landmark.** (page 264)

law

A rule that everyone must follow. Police officers help make sure the **law** is followed. (page 9)

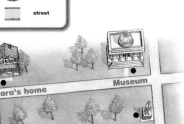

map key

Tells what the symbols on a map stand for. The **map key** helps us read the map. (page 20)

map scale

A tool used to find the distance between two places. We used the **map scale** on our trip. (page 214)

mayor

The leader of a town or city. The **mayor** spoke at the town meeting. (page 155)

monument

A building or statue that honors a person or event. The Lincoln Memorial is a famous **monument.** (page 182)

motto

A word or saying that people try to live by. A **motto** is written on this symbol. (page 181)

natural resource

A useful material that comes from the earth. Soil is a **natural resource.** (page 76)

P

pie chart

A kind of chart that is drawn in the shape of a pie. Matt made a **pie chart** to show how he used his income. (page 130)

pioneer

A person who goes first and prepares the way for others. A **pioneer** needed to work very hard. (page 224)

President

The leader of our country. The **President** gave a speech. (page 168)

producer

Someone who makes or grows something. A farmer is a **producer.** (page 68)

R

route

A way to go from one place to another. This map shows the **route** from the post office to the bank. (page 125)

rural

An area with small communities and open space. The farm is in a **rural** area. (page 26)

services

Jobs that people do to help others. A restaurant worker provides **services.** (page 105)

shelter

A place where people live. People need **shelter.** (page 203)

suburb

A type of community that is located near a city. The **suburb** I live in is close to New York City. (page 25)

symbol

A picture that stands for something. She found the **symbol** for a tree on the map. (page 20)

State	Flag	About the Flag
Texas		This is called the Lone Star Flag.
California		The grizzly bear stands for courage.

table

A kind of list. The **table** showed important information. (page 164)

tax

Money that is collected by a government. Some of our **tax** money will be used to build a new school. (page 113)

time line
Shows the order in which things happen. We made a **time line** about holidays. (page 226)

trade
To buy, sell, or exchange goods. People can **trade** goods at a market. (page 134)

tradition
Something that is done a certain way for many years. Going to a parade on Independence Day is a family **tradition.** (page 207)

transportation
A way of moving goods or people from place to place. An airplane is one kind of **transportation.** (page 135)

urban
A type of area that is made up of a city and the places around it. We just moved to an **urban** area. (page 24)

vote
A choice that gets counted. We **vote** for class president. (page 11)

Index

Factory, 101, 120–124, 142
Family
  ancestors in a, 68
  history, 248–249
Famous People
  Alvarado, Linda, 132–133
  Anthony, Susan B., 178–179
  Banneker, Benjamin, 34–35
  Beavers, Anna, 158
  Carson, Rachel, 86–87
  Carter, Rosalynn, 28–29
  Chavez, Cesar, 74–75
  Clark, William, 222–223, 225, 226–227
  Columbus, Christopher, 210
  Deloria, Ella Cara, 206–207
  Douglass, Frederick, 231
  Earhart, Amelia, 281
  Ford, Henry 280
  Fulton, Robert, 282–283
  Henry, Patrick, 217
  Jefferson, Thomas, 182, 217, 222, 264
  Keller, Helen, 279
  King, Jr., Martin Luther, 183
  L'Enfant, Pierre, 35
  Lewis, Meriwether, 222–223, 225, 226–227
  Lincoln, Abraham, 182, 232–233, 235, 266
  Marshall, Thurgood, 170–171
  Nightingale, Florence, 116–117
  Ochoa, Ellen, 254–255
  O'Connor, Sandra Day, 169
  Pei, I.M., 268–269
  Revere, Paul, 220–221
  Robinson, Jackie, 233
  Roosevelt, Theodore, 266
  Smith, John, 211
  Squanto, 212–213
  Truth, Sojourner, 234–235
  Tubman, Harriet, 231, 233, 234
  Washington, George, H11, 182, 218, 219, 266
  Waste, Anpetu, 206
  Wright Brothers, 281
Farms, 64, 74–75, 79
Flag Day, 240, 256
Flags, 30, 186–187, 191
  countries, 186–187
  United States, 187, 188–189
Florida, 165,
  St. Augustine, 210, 265, 267
  Tallahassee, 164
Folktale
  An Honest Man, 284–285
"Follow the Drinkin' Gourd," 236–237
Food
  as a good, 104
  as a need, 66
  made from flour, 78
Ford, Henry, 280
France, 218, 266, 281
Freedom, 151, 180–183, 190, 196, 217–219, 250
Fulton, Robert, 282–283

Gateway Arch, 265, 267
Geographer, 56
Geography, 52, 56, 59, 92
Geography, themes of, H16–H17
  Location, H16
  Movement, H16
  Place, H16
  Places and People Change Each Other, H17
  Region, H17
Geography, terms, dictionary of, EM
  R10–R11
Georgia, 30, 33, 64, 65
  Atlanta, 33
  Plains, 29
  Statesboro, 64
Geysers, 84
Globe, 37, 38–39
Goods, 71, 100, 104–107, 120–123, 128–129, 134, 138, 142, 145, 146
Government, 150, 162, 190, 193
  federal, 33,166–169
  local, 154–157
  state, 33, 160–163, 164–165
  three parts of, 167–169
Governmental Services
  library, 14–15, 109
  park, 16, 19, 21–22
  school, 10, 11, 158–159, 171
Governor, 150, 160, 162–163, 169, 190
Graphs, 80–81, 94
Great Plains, 67, 78
Great Wall of China, The, 271
Groups
  belonging to, 6–7

Habitat, 89
Harvest, 70–72
Hawaii, 63, 65, 136
  Kauai, 63
Henry, Patrick, 217
Here and There
  Flags Around the World, 186
  Landmarks Around the World, 270
Hieroglyphics, 273
Hill, 57, 61
History, 4, 22–23, 44, 138–139, 228–229, 230–233, 234–236, 244, 248–249, 251–252, 258–259, 262–265, 268–269, 270–273, 277–279, 280–281
Holidays, 247, 256–259, 286, 289
  Cinco de Mayo, 258, 289
  Columbus Day, 257
  Dr. Martin Luther King, Jr., Day, 183, 256
  Election Day, 287
  Flag Day, 240, 256
  Independence Day, 219, 240, 257
  Juneteenth, 259, 289

  Labor Day, 257
  Memorial Day, 240, 256–257, 259
  Mother's Day, 261
  Presidents' Day, 256
  Thanksgiving, 213, 215, 256
  Veterans Day, 257, 287
Homes and Houses
  as a need, 66
  in a neighborhood, 8
  tepees, 67

Illinois, Chicago, 262
Immigrant Wall of Honor, 253
Immigrants, 246, 250–253, 286, 289
Income, 98, 100, 104–106, 126–127, 142
Independence, 199, 217–219, 238
Independence Day, 219, 240, 257
India, 187
Indiana, 191
Inventions, 246, 275, 286
Irrigate, 69, 93
Islands, 58, 63
Italy, Florence, 117

Jefferson Memorial, 182
Jefferson, Thomas, 182, 217, 222, 264
Johnson Space Center, 254
Judges, 156, 169
Junior Ranger, 83–84

Keller, Helen, 279
Kenya, 187
Kids Care Clubs, 12–13
King, Jr., Martin Luther, 183

Labor Day, 257
Lake, 50, 59, 61
Land, to use or change, 68, 71
Landforms, 52, 56–59, 60–61, 92
Landmarks, 246, 264–267, 270–271, 290
  county courthouse, 156
  national capitol building, 167
  state capitol building, 161
Laws, 4, 9, 33, 44, 154, 156, 167–169
L'Enfant, Pierre, 35
Lewis, Meriwether, 222–223, 225, 226–227
Lexington, Massachusetts, 221
Liberty, 181, 196
Liberty Bell, 181

Index

Credits

Dorling Kindersley (DK) is an international publishing company specializing in the creation of high quality reference content for books, CD-ROMs, online materials, and video. The hallmark of DK content is its unique combination of educational value and strong visual style. This combination allows DK to deliver appealing, accessible, and engaging educational content that delights children, parents, and teachers around the world. Scott Foresman is delighted to have been able to use selected extracts of DK content within this Social Studies program.

72–73 from *Farm* by Ned Halley. Copyright © 2000 by Dorling Kindersley Limited.

Photographs: Photo locators are denoted as follows: Top (T), Center (C), Bottom (B), Left (L), Right (R), Background (Bkgd).

Front Matter: E1 (TC) Stockbyte; © Ray F. Hillstrom/The 11th Hour Online; (CL) © Buddy Mays/ Travel Stock; (C) © Lee Foster/Lonely Planet Images; (BL) Milwaukee Department of City Development; © Steve Bloom Images/Alamy.com; (BC) © Peter Beck/Corbis; (TL) © Buddy Mays/ Corbis; E2 (BC) © Richard A. Cooke/Corbis; (BR) © Werner Forman/Art Resource, NY; (T) Getty Images; (Bkgd) Corbis; E3 (TL) © Richard Cummins/Lonely Planet Images; (B) © Buddy Mays/ Corbis; (BR) © Richard A. Cooke/Corbis; E4 (BL) Getty Images; (BC) AP/Wide World Photos; (B) Stockbyte; E5 (CR) Stockbyte; (C) Getty Images; E6 (R) © Peter Schulz/Index Stock Imagery; (L) SuperStock; (Bkgd) © Roger Tully/Getty Images; E7 (BC) AP/Wide World Photos; (CL) © Ray F. Hillstrom/The 11th Hour Online; (BR) Getty Images; E8 (BC) © Steve Allen/Brand X Pictures; (C) © Buddy Mays/Travel Stock; E9 (BL) © Buddy Mays/Corbis; (C) © Bob Krist/Corbis; (BC) Look South; (TC) © Peter Finger/Corbis; (C) © John McAnulty/Corbis; E10 (BR, Bkgd, BL) Getty Images; (BR) © Lee Foster/Lonely Planet Images; E11 (BL) © Rick Olivier; (BC) © Steven Needham/ Envision; (BR) Getty Images; (Bkgd) © Richard T. Nowitz/Corbis; E12 (BR) © Peter Beck/Corbis; (TR) © Steve Bloom Images/Alamy.com; (Bkgd, CL) Getty Images; E13 (C) © Clark James Mishler Photography; (BC, TC) © Brandon Cole Marine Photography/Alamy.com; (BC) © Paul Edmondson/ Getty Images; E14 (BR) Getty Images; (TR) Corbis; (C) Milwaukee Department of City Development; (Bkgd) Getty Images; (Bkgd) © Robert DiGiacomo/Comstock Inc.; E15 (L & R edge) © Chris Abraham/Corbis; (BL) © John Neubauer/PhotoEdit; (BR) Getty Images; E16 (TL) © Lester Lefkowitz/Corbis; (CL) © Steve Bloom Images/Alamy.com; (C) Joseph Sohm; Visions of America/ Corbis; E1 (TL, CL) Getty Images, (TC) © Tom Sayler/ Silver Image, (CL) AP/Wide World Photos, (C) Len Kaufman, (BL) Index Stock Imagery, (BC) ©Nicole Duplaix/Corbis, (BC) © Michael R. Brown/Silver Image, (BC) © Douglas Peebles/Corbis; E2 (CL) Timothy O'Keefe/Index Stock Imagery, (CR) Ah-Tha-Thi-Ki Museum, (T) Jeff Greenberg/The Image Works, Inc., (BR) Tom Sayler/Silver Image; E3 (C) Len Kaufman, (BR) Marilyn "Angel" Wynn/Nativestock; E4 (BR) Fiesta of Five Flags, (CL) Stephen Bond/Alamy.com, (CR) Paul A. Souders/Corbis, (CL) Michael S. Yamashita/Corbis; E5 (TL, TC) Fiesta of Five Flags, (BR) Getty Images, BC) © Bo Zaunders/Corbis; E6 (L) AP/Wide World Photos, (BR) PhotoEdit; E7 (TC) AP/Wide World Photos, (BC, BR) Getty Images, (Bkgd) SuperStock; E8 (C) © Henry C. Aldrich, (C) © Jeff Greenberg/Silver Image, (L, TR, R, Bkgd) Getty Images; E9 (C) Len Kaufman, (TL) Blair Thomas/ Worldcrossings.com, (BC) Mark Barrett/Silver Image; E10 (CR) Pat Canova/Silver Image, (BC) Index Stock Imagery, (TL, C) Getty Images; E11 (TC) Jeff Greenberg/PhotoEdit, (TL) Pat Canova/ Index Stock Imagery, (BR) Corbis, (BC) Stephen Foster Folk Culture Center State Park, (TL) Roman Soumar/Corbis; E12 (CL, BL) Suncoast Seabird Sanctuary, (Bkgd) Corbis, (TC) Craig Tuttle/ Corbis, E13 (CL) James Phillips/Silver Image, (BR) Nicole Duplaix/Corbis; E14 (BC) Robert DiGiacomo/ © Comstock Inc. (Bkgd) Getty Images, (L) Chris Abraham/Corbis, (BC) PhotoDisc, (BC) Michael R. Brown/Silver Image, (Bkgd) Sheriff's Office, City of Jacksonville; E15 (TL) Corbis, (BC) John Neubauer/PhotoEdit, (BR, TL, Bkgd) Getty Images; E16 (C) Douglas Peebles/Corbis, (C) Dennis MacDonald/PhotoEdit H2 (Bkgd) © Charles Thatcher/Getty Images; (C) Eyewire, Inc., (L) Jim Cummins/FPG International LLC, (R) Jim Arbogast/PhotoDisc, H3 (BR) © Comstock Inc., (BC) Britt J. Erlanson-Messens/Image Bank, (BL) Stephen Simpson/FPG International LLC; H4 Corbis; Don Klumpp/Image Bank; H6 Michael Newman/PhotoEdit; H8 (L) Getty Images, (R) © Mark E. Gibson Stock Photography H9 © Ariel Skelley/Corbis; H11 Colonial Williamsburg Foundation; H12 Douglas Slone/Corbis; H20 Getty Images; H22 (TC) Ben Mangor/SuperStock, (C) © James Marshall/Corbis, (BR) Willard Clay Photography, Inc.; H23 (TR) © Jonathon Blair/Corbis, (C) Getty Images. **Unit 1:** 2 Patti McConville/ Image Bank; 4 (BC) Joseph Sohm/Corbis; 5 (T) Joseph Sohm/Corbis, (TC) Jeff Greenberg/ PhotoEdit, (BC) Thomas Hallstein; 8 Michael S. Yamashita/Corbis-Bettmann; 9 (BL) Coco McCoy/Rainbow, (TR) PhotoDisc, (BR) Chris Rogers/Rainbow, (TL) Corbis; 12,13 Kids Care Clubs; 17 (TR) Max Alexander/© Dorling Kindersley, (BR) Ann Stratton/FoodPix; 18 (L) Rich LaSalle/ Stone; 19 (TR) Gail Mooney/Corbis, (CR) Evan Agostini/Liaison Agency; 22 Lake County Museum/ Corbis-Bettmann; 23 SuperStock; 24 (BR) Michael S. Yamashita/Corbis-Bettmann; 25 (Bkgd) Robert Shafer/Stone, (BL) Jeff Greenberg/PhotoEdit; 26 (Bkgd) Bob Daemmrich/Image Works, (C) Paul Redman/Stone; 27 (CR) Peter Pearson/Stone, (TR) Bill Bachmann/PhotoEdit, (CL) Joseph A. Rosen; 29 Corbis; 33 (TR) J. Pickerell/Image Works, (B) Bob Rowan; Progressive Image/Corbis; 35 The Granger Collection, New York; 38 (BL) Corbis, (T) Keren Su/Stone, (BR) D Palais/Art Directors & TRIP Photo Library, (BL) SuperStock, (C) James P. Rowan Stock Photography; 38 (BR) D. Clegg/Art Directors & TRIP Photo Library; 40 Barnabas and Anabel Kindersley/© Dorling Kindersley, Art Directors & TRIP Photo Library; 41 (TL) Barnabas and Anabel Kindersley/© Dorling Kindersley; **Unit 2:** 49, 50, 51 (Bkgd) Frederick D. Atwood; 52 (TL) McCarthy/Corbis/ Corbis Stock Market, (BL) Kunio Owaki/Corbis Stock Market, (CL) Joe Sohm/Image Works, (CL) Prescott & White/Stone; 53 (CR) Joel W. Rogers/Corbis, (TR) Eric Larrayadieu/Stone, (CR) Craig Aurness/Corbis; 55 (BR) Ryan McVay/PhotoDisc; 57 (T) Joe Sohm/Image Works, (C) Yva Momatiuk & John Eastcott/Image Works, (B) Gary Braasch/Woodfin Camp & Associates; 58 (TR) 1995/Charles Feil/Views from Above, (CR) Dean Abramson/Stock, Boston Inc/PictureQuest, (BR) Catherine Karnow/Woodfin Camp & Associates, (BL) Joel W. Rogers/Corbis; 59 (T) Myrleen Ferguson/PhotoEdit, (B) Dan Budnik/Woodfin Camp & Associates; 62 (L) RubberBall Productions/ PictureQuest, (R) David Muench/Corbis; 63 (T) Heather Titus/Stone; 64 (T) Sondra Dawes/Image Works, (B) Yann Arthus-Bertrand/Corbis; 66 (B) Corbis/Corbis-Bettmann, (T) Marilyn "Angel" Wynn/Native Stock; 67 (CR) PhotoDisc, (T) Marilyn "Angel" Wynn/Nativestock; 68 Courtesy Stark Brothers Nurseries; 69 (T) Courtesy Washington Apple Commission, (C) John Heseltine/Corbis, (B) Courtesy Washington Apple Commission; 70 Vincent Dewitt/Stock Boston; 72 (CL, B, TR) © Dorling Kindersley, (C) © Brian Sytnyk/Masterfile Corporation, (R) Musée des Beaux-Arts, Nantes, France/ Giraudon/Bridgeman Art Library; 73 (TL) © Mark Newman/FLPA-Images of Nature, (TR, C, CL, L) © Dorling Kindersley, (R) Holt Studios, (B) © Darrell Gulin/Corbis; 75 (T) Justin Sullivan/AP/Wide World, (B) AP/Wide World; 77 (TR) Dan McCoy/Rainbow; 78 (T) Robert Glusic/PhotoDisc; 81 C Squared Studios/PhotoDisc; 82 National Park Service; 83 (B) George Lepp/Corbis, (T) National Park Service; 84 National Park Service Photo/United States Department of the Interior; 87 George Rinhart/Corbis-Bettmann; 88 (T) Earth Angels/Courtesy Guardian Angel Settlement Association, (BR) Rebecca Shelby/Earth Angels/Courtesy Guardian Angel Settlement Association, (BL) Gary W. Carter/Corbis; 89 (B) Gary W. Carter/Corbis; **Unit 3:** 100 (T) Photolink/PhotoDisc, (TC) Jeffry Myers/Stock Boston, (BC) Photolink/PhotoDisc; 101 (T) Corbis, (BC) Randy Jolly/Image Works; 103 (T) Paul A. Souders/Corbis; 110, 111 Courtesy Phoenix Kids Pride Commission; 114 (C) Jimmy Dorantes/Latin Focus, (B) B. Mahoney/Image Works, (T) Greg Kuchik/Volume Series 43: Business & Occupations/PhotoDisc; 115 (T) R. Lord/Image Works, (B) SuperStock; 118, 119 Aberdeen Fire Department, Maryland/© Dorling Kindersley; 120 Amy C. Etra/PhotoEdit; 121 (C) PhotoDisc, (T) Richard Hamilton Smith/Corbis, (B) Inga Spence/Index Stock Imagery; 122 (TL), (TR), (TC), (BR) Courtesy of National Cotton Council of America; 122 (BL) Courtesy Gaston County Dyeing Machine; 122 (BC) Amy C. Etra/PhotoEdit; 126 Richard Lord/PhotoEdit; 133 Courtesy of Linda Alvarado/Alvarado Construction Inc.; 134 (BR) Michael S. Yamashita/Corbis; 135 (T) Lester Lefkowitz/Corbis Stock Market, (B) Gallo Images/Corbis; 136 Charles O. Cecil/Words & Pictures/ PictureQuest; 138 F.S. Church/North Wind Picture Archives; **Unit 4:** 147 (Bkgd) John Neubauer/ PhotoEdit; 148, 149 (Bkgd) Jeff Greenberg/PhotoEdit; 150 (T) Phillip Gould/Corbis, (TC) N.P. Alexander/Visuals Unlimited, (BC) Daemmrich Photography, (B) Grasser/Mauritius/H. Armstrong Roberts; 151 (TC) The Granger Collection, New York, (T) Vivian Ronay, (C) R. Kord/H. Armstrong Roberts, (BC) The Granger Collection, New York, (BR) David Jennings/Image Works; 156 W.J. Scott/H. Armstrong Roberts; 158, 159 Courtesy, Anna Beavers; 164 (TL) Jeff Greenberg/Visuals Unlimited, (TC) Mary Ann McDonald/Visuals Unlimited, (TR) William J. Weber/Visuals Unlimited, (CL) SuperStock; (BL) © Lee Snider/Corbis; (CC) © Arthur Morris/Visuals Unlimited; (BR) Getty Images; (CR) © David Sieren/Visuals Unlimited; (BR) © 1997 Alan & Linda Detrick/Photo Researchers, Inc.; 167 (T) Mark Wilson/Newsmakers/Liaison, (B) Tom McCarthy/PhotoEdit; 168 (B) Dennis O'Clair/Stone; 169 (B) Fred Ward/Black Star, (T) Lee Snider/ Corbis; 171 (T) Bettman Archives/Corbis-Bettmann, (B) Corbis-Bettmann; 176 AP/Wide World Photos 177 Colonial Williamsburg Foundation; 179 (T) Corbis-Bettmann, (B) TimePix; 182 (CL) Hisham F. Ibrahim/PhotoDisc, (T) Museum of the City of New York/Corbis, (BL) D. Gaudette/ Stone, (BR) Corbis-Bettmann, (CC) David Jennings/Image Works, (CR) Bettmann/Corbis; 183 (Bkgd) Archive Photos; **Unit 5:** 195 (Bkgd) Robert Glusic/PhotoDisc; 196 (L) The Newark Museum/Art Resource, NY, (BC) The Purcell Team/Corbis, (TC) The Newark Museum/Art Resource, NY, (R) The Newark Museum/Art Resource, NY; 198 (T) John Elk III/Stock Boston, (BC), (B) The Granger Collection, New York, (TC) Bill Ross/Corbis; 199 (T), (B) The Granger Collection, New York, (C) N. Carter/North Wind Picture Archives; 203 (TL) Phyllis Picardi/Stock Boston, (TCL) Jamestown Yorktown Foundation, Williamsburg, VA (TCR) Marilyn "Angel" Wynn, (TR) The Granger Collection, New York, (CL) Momatiuk/Eastcott/Woodfin Camp & Associates, (CCL) Marilyn "Angel" Wynn, (CCR) Corbis, (CR) North Wind Picture Archives, (BL) Reinhard Brucker/ Westwind Enterprises, (BCL) Werner Forman Archive/Arizona State Museum/Art Resource, NY, (BCR) David Weintraub/Stock Boston, (BR) 1995–2001 Denver Public Library, Western History Collection/Library of Congress; 204 (TR), (BL) Marilyn "Angel" Wynn, (BR), (TL) Reinhard Brucker/ Westwind Enterprises; 205 (T) North Wind Picture Archives, (B) Buddy Mays/Corbis; 206 (BR) Dakota Indian Foundation, (BL) Reinhard Brucker/Westwind Enterprises, Werner Forman Archive/Field Museum of Natural History, Chicago, USA/Art Resource, NY; 207 (CR) Dakota Indian Foundation, (BR) Reinhard Brucker/Westwind Enterprises; 208–209 Colonial Williamsburg Foundation; 210 (TL) Archivo Iconografico, S.A./Corbis, (BL) North Wind Picture Archives, (BR) N. Carter/North Wind Picture Archives; 211 Hulton Getty/Stone; 212 (T) The Granger Collection, New York, (B) North Wind Picture Archives; 213 (T) Tom McCarthy/PhotoEdit, (B) PhotoDisc; 215 © Roman Soumar/Corbis/Bettmann; 216 The Granger Collection, New York; 217 Stock Montage Inc.; 218 (B) Stock Montage Inc., (T) Museum of the City of New York/Corbis; 221 (T) Michael A. Dwyer/Stock Boston, (B) The Granger Collection, New York; 222 Marilyn "Angel" Wynn/ Nativestock; 223 North Wind Picture Archives; 227 (L) Corbis (R) The Granger Collection, New York; 229 (T) Archive Photos, (C) David Ulmer/Stock Boston, (B) Art Resource, NY; 230 The Granger Collection, New York; 231 Corbis-Bettmann; 232 (BL) Bettmann/Corbis, (BR) The Granger Collection, New York; 233 (T) The Granger Collection, New York, (B) Corbis-Bettmann; 235 (T) Hulton Getty Picture Library/Stone; 240 (L) AP/Wide World, (R) Kevin Fleming/Corbis; **Unit 6:** 243 (Bkgd) M. Lee/Art Directors & TRIP Photo Library, (B) Austrian Archives/Corbis; 244 (Bkgd) Michael S. Yamashita/Corbis, (BR) Eyewire, Inc.; 245 (TR) Bob Krist/Corbis, (TL) Latin Focus, (BR) Horace Bristol/Corbis, (BL) Austrian Archives/Corbis; 246 (TL) California State Parks, (BC) Spencer Grant/PhotoEdit, (TC) Joel Sartore/Grant Heilman Photography, (B) C. Borland/ PhotoLink/PhotoDisc; 247 (C) Gemma Giannini/Grant Heilman Photography, (T) The Granger Collection, New York; 248, 249 (Bkgd) PhotoDisc; 251 (T) Corbis-Bettmann, (B) Catherine Ursillo/ Photo Researchers, Inc.; 252 (T) The Granger Collection, New York, (B) David Ryan/Photo 20-20/PictureQuest; 253 Jeff Greenberg/PhotoEdit; 254 (BR) Corbis, (L) NASA/Photo Researchers, Inc.; 255 NASA; 256 (BR) Corbis-Bettmann, (BL) Flip Schulke/Corbis, (TC) Stock Montage, Inc.; 257 (BL) Kevin Fleming/Corbis, (BC) Spencer Grant/PhotoEdit, (TL) Corbis-Bettmann, (TR) Rhoda Sidney/PhotoEdit, (BR) Steve Cole/PhotoDisc; 258 (BL) Daemmrich Photography, (BR) Brenda Tharp/Photo Researchers, Inc., (T) © Bob Daemmrich/Stock Boston; 259 (T) Daemmrich Photography, (B) The UT Institute of Texan Cultures at San Antonio; 260, 261 Barnabas Kindersley/© Dorling Kindersley; 264 (L) Corbis-Bettmann, (R) Kevin Horan/Stock Boston; 265 (T) David Muench/Corbis, (BR) D. Boone/Corbis, (BL) © Steve Vidler/SuperStock; 266 (B) R. Morley/ PhotoLink/PhotoDisc, (TR) Bill Ross/Corbis, (TL) C. Borland/PhotoLink/PhotoDisc; 267 (TC) Kevin Horan/Stock Boston, (BC) David Muench/Corbis, (BL) D. Boone/Corbis, (C) (BR) © Steve Vidler/ SuperStock, (BR) R. Morley/PhotoLink/PhotoDisc, (TR) Bill Ross/Corbis, (TL) C. Borland/PhotoLink/ PhotoDisc; 269 (T) Ellis Herwig/Stock Boston, (B) Owen Franken/Corbis; 270 Charles Preitner/ Visuals Unlimited; 271 Peter Menzel/Stock Boston; 272 (BC) H. Rogers/Art Directors & TRIP Photo Library, (TC), (TL) The Granger Collection, New York, (BR) H. Rogers/Art Directors & TRIP Photo Library, (BL) P. Belzeaux/Photo Researchers, Inc., (TR) Photo Researchers, Inc.; 273 (T) Rudi von Briel/PhotoEdit,(B) Jack Fields/Corbis; 274 (BR) H. Rogers/Art Directors & TRIP Photo Library, (BL) Corbis-Bettmann, (T) Lloyd Cluff/Corbis; 275 (L) Gemma Giannini/Grant Heilman Photography, (T) Bill Gallery/Stock Boston, (R) Farrell Grehan/Photo Researchers, Inc.; 276 Charles Preitner/Visuals Unlimited ; 278 Michael Newman/PhotoEdit; 279 (R) Lloyd Cluff/Corbis, (L) Will & Deni McIntyre/ Photo Researchers, Inc.; 280 (T) Ewing Galloway/Index Stock Imagery, (B) Hulton-Deutsch Collection/Corbis; 281 (R) Corbis-Bettmann; 283 (B) Corbis-Bettmann; 287 Steve Cole/PhotoDisc **End Matter:** R12 (T) Prescott & White/Stone, (B) Buddy Mays/Corbis; R13 (TC) Daemmrich Photography, (BC), (C) The Granger Collection, New York, (B) Joseph Sohm/Corbis, (T) J. Pickerell/Image Works; R14 (T) Vivian Ronay, (TC) Eric Larrayadieu/Stone, (BC) Craig Aurness/ Corbis, (B) Spencer Grant/Photoedit, (BL) Charles Preitner/Visuals Unlimited; R15 (T) The Granger Collection, New York, (C) R. Kord/H. Armstrong Roberts, (B) Phillip Gould/Corbis, (BC) Jeffry Myers/Stock Boston, (TC) Corbis; R16 (BC) Tom McCarthy/PhotoEdit, (TC) Colonial Williamsburg Foundation, (B) California State Parks, (T) Grasser/Mauritius/H. Armstrong Roberts; R17 (TC) N. Carter/North Wind Picture Archives, (T) Photolink/PhotoDisc, (C) Gemma Giannini/Grant Heilman Photography, (CL)Joe Sohm/Image Works; R18 (BC) The Granger Collection, New York, (B) Joel W. Rogers/Corbis, (T) N.P. Alexander/Visuals Unlimited; R19 (T), (TC) The Granger Collection, New York, (BC) Kunio Owaki/Corbis Stock Market, (B) Thomas Hallstein; R20 (TC) John Elk III/Stock Boston, (T) Photolink/PhotoDisc; R21 (BC) Randy Jolly/Image Works, (TL) AP/Wide World, (TR) Kevin Fleming/Corbis, (TC) Bill Ross/Corbis